Singing
an
ABC

Singing Bowls:
an
ABC

Geert Verbeke

PILGRIMS

PILGRIMS PUBLISHING
◆ Varanasi ◆

SINGING BOWLS : AN ABC
Geert Verbeke

Published by:
PILGRIMS PUBLISHING

An imprint of:
PILGRIMS BOOK HOUSE
(Distributors in India)
B 27/98 A-8, Nawabganj Road
Durga Kund, Varanasi-221010, India
Tel: 91-542-2314059, 2314060, 2312456
Fax: 91-542-2312788, 2311612
E-mail: pilgrims@satyam.net.in
Website: www.pilgrimsbooks.com

PILGRIMS BOOK HOUSE (New Delhi)
9 Netaji Subhash Marg, 2nd Floor
Near Neeru Hotel, Daryaganj, New Delhi 110002
Tel: 91-11-23285081
E-mail: pilgrim@del2.vsnl.net.in

Distributed in Nepal by:
PILGRIMS BOOK HOUSE
P O Box 3872, Thamel, Kathmandu, Nepal
Tel: 977-1-4700942, Off: 977-1-4700919
Fax: 977-1-4700943
E-mail: pilgrims@wlink.com.np

Second Edition Revised and Corrected Copyright © 2005
Copyright © 2000, by Pilgrims Publishing for India and Nepal
All Rights Reserved
Copyright © Geert Verbeke
Edited by Sian Pritchard-Jones
Photographs and illustrations by Geert Verbeke

ISBN: 81-7769-223-2

Printed in India at Pilgrim Press Pvt. Ltd. Lalpur Varanasi

Dedicated to

My beloved 'soulsister' Jenny Ovaere for precious love & the whole ABC.
My peculiar kids: Hans, Saskia, Merlijn & Jonas, sparks of the divine fire.
Shaman, honourable sound therapist, friend and bowl master, Joska Soos.
The Anonymous Himalayan Bowlsmiths.

In Memoriam

My parents Walter Verbeke and Jo Hiltrop, mirrors of my inner being.
My spiritual guides Pietro Bares, Osho and J. Krishnamurti.
Gerard de Backer (passed away on 28 August 1999), for his hearty gift of my first singing bowl...
Walter De Vos (passed away on 13 July 1999).

In Memoriam

Acknowledgements

This modest lexicon only exists as a product of the communication with generous friends who have inspired me with their love, resources and criticism. From all of them, I had much to learn! For each I have a unique feeling of gratitude and a warm appreciation:

Mr. Rama Nand Tiwari of Pilgrim Books House in Thamel, Kathmandu, Nepal.

My editors, Mr. Chaitanya Nagar, Siân Pritchard-Jones and Bob Gibbons.

Mr. Nagendra Singh and the whole staff of Pilgrims Book House.

Annita Deweer for first proof reading, text improvements and amendments.

Paiste, Switzerland for information about cymbals & gongs.

Vera Broos & Hugo Ingels... fly me to the moon!

Our friends in the USA: Arjen van den Eerenbeemt, Shirley & Bob Staelens, Cozette & Terry Schenks, Debra & Randy Ramsley, Alexander & Françoise Lepers.

Franz & Elli Biehal (Wien), for wine and the camper-concert at Canyon Lands.

Fred van Hove, Gilbert Isbin, Wim Vandekerckhove, Norbert Detaeye, Colin Offord & Stephan Micus for what we have in common: investigation into new sounds.

Marie-Jeanne Budé, Mon van der Biest and Marc Ostermeyer, for Himalayan bowls & support in a kindred spirit.

Yanto van den Heuvel and Kees Kort for Empty Sky.

Paul Duboccage: Boum... Shankar!

Jacques Germonprez & Trees Gits, for love.

Ivan Candaele & Dirk D'Hondt, high & dry in the Highgate...

Christina de Kaste, Fons Bertels & all the other singing bowl lovers...

My Friends, Wisdom's Daughters and you...

"If the music of a Kingdom changes, its society will alter itself"—*Confucius*

Foreword

When I first visited Nepal in 1974 the valley was very rural; one only had to walk a kilometre from Kathmandu Durbar Square to be in countryside dotted with farms and pastoral scenes. In the squares of the old city, musicians played each night while cows, chickens and pigs rummaged among the natural waste in the streets. Kathmandu was a city of artisans.

One was immediately struck by the number of craftsmen busy in the narrow alleys of Patan, Bhaktapur and Kathmandu. Amongst the craftsmen would be metal workers making bowls; some would become singing bowls. Times change, some things improve, some things are lost. The city is healthier, but not always cleaner. Tourists have less 'singing bowels' and more money. There has been a great awakening in things Hindu, Buddhist and Tibetan, and a new spiritual awareness has grown among visitors.

Many new books have been published about these ancient ideas and practices. The use of singing bowls has become more widely recognised and this book helps to enlighten the interested reader about their many varied functions in making music, healing and spiritual awakening.

A portion of the proceeds from the sale of this book will be donated to a fund for 'Clean up Kathmandu'.

Introduction

Namaste, I honour the light within you. Playing with the unusual bowls and gongs provided inspiration for this lexicon. It is the result of travels, many conversations, meetings, concerts, readings and a personal odyssey into the wonderful world of sound and singing bowls. The purpose of this book is to provide basic information about singing bowls, it is not meant to be definitive. Many people have become familiar with singing bowls, now for sale in different sizes and alloys. More knowledge and useful information is coming to light, more details are discovered, with mysterious quotations, secret stories and juicy information.

Springtime 1993, a wonderful, spirit-filled, sound sings and creates sacred space. I am surrounded by several bronze-coloured bowls. Gerard de Backer knocks the rim of a twelve-inch singing bowl with a crooked wand bandaged with tape. Overtones pulsate brightly and envelop my body. This sound-experience is new, as if the tones come out of my soul to stabilise my feelings and emotions. Gerard offers me my first singing bowl...

Now, the experiments with the bowls go on. Meanwhile my first bowl, with Devangiri-inscription, was singing at the

Chartres cathedral, the winterchurch of Chevetogne. Also in a pleasure aircraft in the Empty Sky of Flanders, in the silence of the Aya Sophia in Istanbul and in the National Parks of Arizona, Utah and Colorado. Gathering the material for this book has made me more mindful that we are part of each other and the whole spiritual world. Nothing gets lost! To everyone who ever heard the Singing of the Sacred Himalayan Bowls: Peace!

Chieftain Seattle of the Dwamisch Indians asked in 1854: "How can someone possess the air?"...
He that nothing questions, nothing learns?

—*Geert Verbeke*, Kortrijk, Flanders 2000.

Preface

Fascination and perception grow in a personal relationship with the wonderful singing bowls. The techniques in this book were certainly not invented by the author. As a matter of fact, they could hardly be the intellectual property of one person, because they are incontestably the final result of the cross-pollination of ancient therapeutic and cultural traditions.

Beautiful tones, with unique tonal colourations, have a direct relationship with each other. Planets move in their orbits, each one emitting their own tone and sound. All universes are filled with energies from the creative sound. Sound belongs, just as silence, to everyone. The whole cosmos is one vibration, one powerful sound. We are all instruments, even entire symphonies. Let's consider ourselves as charming instruments. How are we playing? Every method or therapist who claims the rules on how to handle the singing bowls, is wrong. To carry out music or relaxation according to a prescribed technique - even when approved, contemporary and noble - means a degradation into a mechanical fact. Be your own prophet! Picked up, here and there, a few workshops can help you to discover the real nature and the spirit of the singing bowls. Personal effort, independent experiments and an open mind are preferable to acquired tricks. Be your own pupil. When the disciple is ready, the Master will appear!

I can not deny that singing bowls are connected with the history of civilisation. No one, in particular, is their inventor or thief. An open mind and a considerable measure of scepsis are indispensable.

If you are a newcomer, take your time, start with the beginning! He that would pick the fruit, must climb the tree... My own early days with a few bowls and one gong, now eight years ago, were full of exploring how to learn as much as I could about the sounds and effects of singing bowls. 'Learning' is still a beautiful keyword on my exciting paths. I hope that you, eager to learn, will find something of interest in 'Singing Bowls ABC'. May some suggestions and remarks broaden your musical horizons. Let's hope meanwhile that what began as just another hobby will become more and more an essential part of your creativity, and that your love affair with the bowls will be something more than a passing fancy.

So far, so good. You are the one to do the job. Fumble your own way and follow the wondering paths of the Himalayan bowls as a lone student. I really don't know if there are any golden keys or magic words to play the bowls. There are perhaps tutors on the (New Age) market who will promise to teach you to play the Himalayan bowls in a short time (and for a lot of money). Sorry, it takes time... and don't even think of playing simple song accompaniments. There are no chords, no chord symbols and no repertoires in different keys. Clearly singing bowls cannot be tuned. It's impossible to play "The Yellow Submarine" or "Jailhouse Rock."

Your own Bowl:

"The sound of your love is even more important than the sound of any bowls."
Shaman Joska Soos

Don't think that you are too clumsy to play the bowls; anyone can learn how to work with them. Just remember that any patent or copyright about bowl-techniques is out of the question. "You are a light for yourself," says Buddha. Mankind looks for his own mirror image in the world of sounds. Nomadic smiths of the Himalayas understand the language of fire, water, air and earth. Metals greet each other in peculiar and wonderful overtones. Shamans and Buddhists hold up a magical mirror. Holy sounds are hidden in the singing bowls. Every bowl has its own story, unclear and vague about its origin. All bowls have mysterious spiritual sounds and vibrations. On this point, sometimes the explanation of traders and merchants is plausible, often full of imagination and irrelevant or even untrue and belonging to 'Absurdistan'. Every bowl has its own character, musical setting, vibrations and sounds. The ability of these sounds to positively or negatively influence health, character, morality and consciousness has been known since ancient times.

Bowls of varying types, as well as certain tingshaws or bells, can be used to help your ability to meditate or to reach higher spiritual levels. For this purpose, it is essential that you choose a bowl and make it your own. Your meditation bowl is yours.

It should not be handled by other people. This kind of bowl can be, more than you expect, a special friend. It will help you to attract and release cosmic energies and to reach deeper states of meditation, increase spiritual awareness, awakening and consciousness. The sounds and vibrations that your meditation bowl produces will relax your mind and keep your feelings clear and fresh. There is no right or wrong way. Let your ears, and heart, tell you what to do! Believe them and enjoy a good spiritual sound-trip. Your master lives in you. Relaxation means exploration. Tune in on the harmony inside yourself. Sound occurring in your body and soul trembles through every fibre. Love on the first hearing. Sound fever!

> To my mind, there cannot be any doubt that the so-called Tibetan singing bowls really do exist.
>
> *—An expert*

> To my mind, there cannot be any doubt that the so-called Tibetan singing bowls really don't exist.
>
> *—Another expert*

> The sound of your love is even more important than the sound of any bowl.
>
> *—Shaman Joska Soos,*
> *Duffel, 1999*

> I am the master of sound.
> Through sound I can kill what lives
> and bring back to life what is dead.
>
> *—Ancient Lama Saying*

A

Abundance (and Richness):

Certainly, the connotation that bowls 'provide abundance and richness', will be most welcome in the mind of many (New Age) traders, all over the world, who exaggerate the qualities of their singing bowls through esoteric thumb-sucking. The expression 'spiritual supermarket' flew off the pen of the American journalist Robert Greenfield. He wrote about the hundreds of gurus, swamis, faith-healers, aura-readers, self-appointed gods and soul-saviours, who present not only bowls and clairaudience, but also themselves for sale with the new Millennium in mind. Clairaudience is the hearing of sounds, music and voices not audible to 'our' normal hearing.

Adding of Toneless Vowels:

Miming or singing toneless vowels against the rim of your bowl can make peculiar sounds and vibrations. Sounds taken into your oral cavity will modulate in pitch with beautiful overtones. This unfathomable sound is related to Mongolian overtone-singing with vocalised ornamentation, Buddhist temple-songs and the trance-traditions of Shamans. Voices have a tremendous ability to be instruments for relaxation and healing. That's the magic in music and sounds.

Adding of Water:

You can hear soft glissandi from various parts of a bowl. An exceptional sound can be realised. Tip a bowl, which has been beaten, so that a small amount of water can elicit a wide range of wonderful and sparkling overtones. Admire also the geometric shapes, which look like meditation-images or Yantras, appearing in the water. As a medium, water vibrates easily. The result of beating or rubbing the rim of a bowl full of water, can be a dazzling and brilliant fountain.

A singing bowl (metal or silica), one-third filled with clear and fresh water, can be used to create flower-essences and elixirs. You don't even need alchemy or astrology. Put the bowl in sunlight (or moonlight) in order to charge the water with magical power. Sound the bowl from time to time.

In his marvellous composition 'Magnificent Meditation' on his recommended CD 'Savage Silence' (Keytone Records-KYT795), Dries Langeveld uses the slapping glissandos of water in a singing bowl to saturate the thinking process. After a while, you stop thinking and go beyond emptiness. The cleansing feeling stays with you for a while after his music has stopped.

Affirmations:

Affirmations are mental medicines that give power to this thinking and feeling. With a few bowls it is possible to employ a more concentrated focus on your spiritual message. The intention of your affirmations is to empower the force of a positive wish or a message. Affirmations can be used in long-distance-healing by sending prayers and healing to others. Read your affirmation and let the sound-resonating bring over your message.

It's good to have a positive mental attitude when starting and ending an affirmation session with your bowls. About this ethical subject it is always good to affirm that you keep in mind the highest good of all. Indeed, you have not the right to influence the free will of other men. This necessary and well-considered attitude needs a serious reflection about the 'New Age' world with its self-satisfied and so called ' Clairvoyant Masters'...

A few Modest Affirmations:

> I feel silence in my inner temple,
> through this peace
> I wish love for the whole world.
> Bring my compassion,
> on your singing tones,
> to the house of who call himself my enemy.
> Affirm with each bowl massage
> the old message:
> "I'm treating people, not diseases."

Age of Aquarius:

For many people this is a supposed two-thousand-year-long era of enlightenment, brotherhood of man, peace and closeness to God(s). The Age of Aquarius is heralded by the entry of the sun into the zodiac sign of Aquarius. As usual in the New Age, astrologers disagree on the exact start. The well-known medium Edgar Cayce (USA), called by some "the Prophet of the New Age", said that these transitions can not be fully understood until the beginning of the twenty-first century in 2001. The supposed transition to Aquarius will bring to our world a change in social and spiritual behaviour. We must wait and see...

Age of the Bowls:

The age of singing bowls is difficult to discover, there are a lot of contradictions. The honourable soundmaster and shaman Joska Soos (born 21st December 1921 at Apostag, Hungaria, now living near Antwerp), wrote in his book(1985) "I am not healing, I am restoring harmony" He was told in 1981 in London some secrets about singing bowls by Tibetan Karmapa monks. Joska Soos is clear in his opinion: "Singing bowls are very old, much older than Lamaism. Scientific research proves that the original bowls date from 2400 years before Christ."

Ted Andrews (USA), author of Animal-speak, Sacred Sounds and Magical Dance, is also a teacher of metaphysical subjects. He refers in his book 'Crystal Balls & Crystal Bowls' to the fact that Tibetan bowls are known for their exotic sounds, which hover in the air long after they have been played. He also mentions that many of the singing bowls are forty to fifty years old and were made by Buddhist priests, prior to the Chinese takeover of Tibet, but the bowls themselves date back centuries in their use. In his vision, the manner in which the metals are combined is secret, for all the originals are handmade. Today bowl masters are no longer allowed to participate in this practice; the Chinese occupiers consider such a 'frivolous' use of minerals and metals.

Alcoholic Excesses:

From singing bowls to 'swinging' bowls? Katzenjammer (Denmark). Katerigheid (Flanders), a hangover is not an immediate invitation to put a bowl on your head! The liver can tolerate a lot but there are limits. Cheers! You should not receive or give relaxation in these circumstances.

Alloy:

The alloy of the bowls is a controversial point. A dissenting meaning talks about seven metals (in India: Sapta Dhatu), connected to seven astrological planets: Gold (Sun), Iron (Mars), Copper (Venus), Mercury (Mercury), Lead (Saturn), Tin (Jupiter) and Silver (Moon). Nickel, Zinc and Antimony are also mentioned instead of Mercury, Lead and Tin. Some sources claim nine metals. At that moment Copper is split up into Red and Yellow Copper; the ninth metal is in this opinion a rare meteorite.

A bowl man, at Durbar Square in Kathmandu, claims to know more about singing bowls and their variety of forms, ornamentation and alloys. He warns that the alloy of a real singing bowl should consist of only five metals: - Bronze (earth), Red Copper (moon & stars), Iron (fire), Silver (air) and Yellow Copper (sun).

This man also warns of bowl replicas, for tourism and cheap trading. In his view, bowls are currently manufactured in the north-central quarter of Patan and the villages of Bhojpur and Chainpur in eastern Nepal. The alloy of these fake bowls also contains gold, lead, zinc and tin, which means that the sacral forces have disappeared. The truth of his statements has yet to be checked and confirmed.

Alpha-Stim 100:

The Alpha-Stim 100, recognised by the American Food and Drug Administration, is a kind of 'walkman' connected by two electric wires to the earlobes to send a light-surge through the brain. The result, after just one hour of 'Alpha-Stimming', is an open and free mind, without allergic reactions or depression. The American inventors suggest that their Alpha-Stim 100 can restore the mind and attitude of drug addicts. I prefer a singing bowl on my head!

Alpha Waves:

It's obvious that mankind responds to the energy of sound. A screaming ambulance siren has a different effect from that of a nightingale singing by moonlight. Classical music has a different effect from that of hard-core punk. Science has confirmed that music, as an organised form of sound, can directly affect mood, brain waves, the nervous system and the body chemistry. Music plays a key role in the religious and spiritual rituals of many cultures. Sound is often considered to be a relaxing and healing salve. So called New Age medicine and dentistry use music primarily to calm and relax patients. Music therapists recognise that some people require stimulating music to energise them towards better health.

Singing bowls produce exceptional and powerful sounds that execute curative and healthy work in spiritual transformation. The micro-electric Alpha waves are especially active. These slow mind waves evoke mostly daydreams, figurative thinking and pure relaxation. Most of the waves of singing bowls demonstrate the same waves as the patterns of the Cerebral Alpha waves. The alpha level is characterised by brain waves of 8 to 13 cycles per second (Hertz). Characteristics are eyes closed, body relaxed, also daydreaming with eyes open. As the music of singing bowls washes through you, it brings your whole body into an alpha state, providing deep rest for all your organs and brain. Bowls have been tested and shown to calm, with alpha brain waves associated with a relaxed and alert state of mind.

The scientist/doctor Richard Gerber (World Research Foundation in Sherman Oaks, USA) suggests that sound therapy is a prototypical energetic healing system. Brainmachines with alpha waves provide relaxation; tetra-waves provide creative daydreams.

Here we can refer to the right cerebral hemisphere as the seat of dreams and intuition. Singing bowls bring the left and right hemisphere into harmony. Don't let your mind be distracted, not even by your own discoveries. Receive, with gratitude, all your inventions about the colour and characters of sounds. The timbre of Singing Bowls is a marked quality with very peculiar characterisation. The wealth of overtones is harmonic. The sound passes, after beating or striking the bowl, through the whole spectrum of clear and metallic to dark and warm. Every bowl has its own timbre and frequency, keynote and overtones.

You have to turn to your own experiences to see how singing bowls affect you.. Let sound be a gate to the conscious world of silence. You don't need to travel, you are already at home.

Amethyst:

Amethyst is a special spiritual stone. A cluster of amethyst in your music room or relaxation chamber is one of the most suitable crystals for your spiritual way. Inner calmness in times of grief and higher wisdom are supported by amethyst.

Animal Spirits:

Animals are invested with spiritual significance, they have much to teach us. Animal spirits can help men with their typical talents and forces. Shamans invoke animal spirits to help them with ceremonies and rites of passage.

Read the exciting book 'Animal- Speak' of author and teacher in the metaphysical and spiritual fields, Ted Andrews, who conducts seminars, symposiums and workshops on many facets of ancient mysticism. His book is a must for everyone who wants to know more about the spiritual and magical powers of creatures great and small. The book includes a comprehensive dictionary of animal, bird and reptile symbolism.

His other books 'Sacred Sounds' and ' Crystal Balls & Crystal Bowls' reveal sound as a direct link between humanity and the divine and how to tap into the magical and healing aspects of voice, resonance and music.

Anti-Stress:

A bowl massage can work against stress and nervous breakdown. Nobody reacts in the same way. Let the recipient lay down on his (her) back. Put a little singing bowl on his (her) forehead and one on his (her) throat. Use a rubber sealing-ring under the bowl to prevent it slipping away.

Let a medium-sized bowl simultaneously vibrate on his (her) hands.

Appellation:

Over the years, bowls have been described by various names— Tibetan bowls, Newari bowls, Buddhist bowls, nomadic bowls, sacred bowls, singing bowls, divine bowls, healing bowls, star bowls, speaking bowls, sacrificial dishes. Also offertory dishes, eating bowls, food dishes, shamanistic bowls, spiritual bowls, skull-shaped bowls, master bowls, monk bowls, mystery bowls, harmonising bowls, chalices, offer bowls. Disrespectful people even talk about folklore bowls.

Atlantis:

The origin of crystal bowls, according to some, leads back to the temple-priests and the travelling healers of the fabled (?) island-continent Atlantis. Colour, light, magnetism and sound were indispensable in this soft and ancient medical science. Whether this information is correct or based on outdated evidence and disproved facts is difficult to answer. These facts apply very well today to the information that 'New Age' supplies. Some 'New Age philosophers' such as Edgar Cayce or Rudolf Steiner propose that our era and the golden age of Atlantis are each other's mirror image.

Let's hope that we still find ourselves in the lucky position that Atlantis or Mu are not an obliging dogma of any fanatic or intolerant doctrine. But even when mankind is free of obligations, the old story of a drowned Atlantis contains a warning against abuse of technology, energy and knowledge.

Auto-Relaxation:

Sit down in front of your favourite singing bowl; let your hands caress the wall. Breathe peacefully. Throw open your mind for the being of the bowls. Let images and emotions get through your soul. Keep breathing peacefully. Thank your singing bowls when there is silence in the big fuss of your mind. Set your mind free, in remembrance of Naropa's words: "My mind is the perfect Buddha, my speech is the perfect teaching, my body is the perfect spiritual community," and open your eyes.

Hold a small bowl close to your hand. Lie down and strike the rim of your bowl. Open your mind and heart.

Lie down with a bowl on your stomach or chest. Strike the bowl gently. Listen and listen again. Taste the inner silence. A vibrating bowl on your open hands gives energy.

Encircle your eyes with a small bowl. Vary from time to time with a splash of water to remove tiredness. Wads with rose-water on the eyelids are celestial. Unless you prefer cucumber slices.

A little bowl on the forehead, third eye, wakes up and can dispel a headache. However, be careful with a continuous headache because it can be the signal for worse complaints, when you should consult a doctor.

A Himalayan bowl, struck gently, upside down on your own head gives an easy manner. It is still a comic sight for the unexpected visitor...

Singing along with a singing bowl is an amusing and pleasant way to discover the world of sounds and relaxation. Try out short and long vocal vowels as a, e, i, o, u. And aa, ee, oe, oo, uu...Humming gives also a pleasant result. Sing 'Aum' (which sounds like 'ohm'). This is a Hindu mantra, comparable with 'Amen' in Hebrew and Christian rites.

Balancing:

A conscious relationship with sounds is the best way to come home in your own life. Discover how listening provides the art of silence. Inner experience lets you see through sounds. Here the right cerebral hemisphere can be referred to as the seat of dreams and intuition. Singing bowls bring the left and right hemisphere into a more balanced phase, by bringing them together in harmony. Don't let your mind be distracted, not even by your own discoveries. The wealth of overtones is harmonic.

Beating:

It is possible to make a great deal of noise with singing bowls. A lot of people have the idea that the louder they play the famous Himalayan bowls, the more 'beat' they will have. Forget it! Noise is not music. A good singing bowl performance is spoilt by playing too loudly; a bad concert can be made even worse. There's absolutely no sense in delivering a heart attack to your audience. A singing bowl is not a noisy hard-core drum but a particularly well-balanced anti-stress instrument.

After beating or striking the bowl, the sound passes through the whole spectrum from clear and metallic to dark and warm.

Every bowl has its own timbre and frequency, keynotes and overtones. Bowls are fellow travellers on a spiritual trip. Let sound be a gate to the conscious world of silence. Play at a reasonable volume, with warm sounds and superior accents.

When struck as a bell with a 'wand' or striker, each bowl has its own predominant sounds and vibrations.

Hit the bowls with a wand or mallet made of hardwood furnished with a strip of felt. Hit the rim high and square. Right-handed people hit at three o'clock, left-handed people hit at nine o'clock. Be sure that your attack is light and soft. Don't use metal mallets.

Be careful in the application of wooden sticks. Avoid playing the inside of a Himalayan bowl.

A bowl hit with fingernails sounds disappointed. A bowl hit with fingers sounds dull.

Only hit or strike a silica bowl with a mallet equipped with felt or with rubber, or a specially developed wand.

The high energy of singing bowls can also be used to charge and clean precious stones and minerals, amulets and talismen or good-luck charms. Put the object(s) in a bowl and sound the bowl from time to time.

Bells:

A Tibetan bell (Dril Bhu or Ghanta) is a symbol of wisdom (pranja), transitory, and the female aspect of energies. The dorje (Thunderbolt) is a symbol of the male aspect, it is always in a set with the bell to restore male and female energies in our body, mind and soul. The set is used traditionally in Buddhist pujas (praying rituals) by monks.

Encircle the bell; play by running the wand along the edge. The friction between the wand (male) and the bell (female) creates an undulating vibration and long-drawn-out singing sound.

By running a piece of wood around the rim of the bell in a circular motion, you build up a singing drone. This prolonged sound is really impressive and penetrating in a church or temple. Additional voices, singing the 'Aum' or 'Amen' sound, will complete this small wonder.

Bells or clocks with an integral sound mechanism were already known 900 years before our calendar. They bring us the sound of the wind. Bells of metal are common, mostly untuned. Bells of ceramic, glass and porcelain are mostly only decorative.

Since ancient times bells have been used as signalling instruments. For example: - the cluster of bells in sacred services, a cycle bell, a school handbell and the town crier or bellman. Many cultures have a bell tree, including Japan. This was used by Shinto dancers in Shinto shrines.

In the sixteenth century, the Turkish Crescent (Jingling Johnny or Chapeau Chinois) was acquired by European regiments. This spectacular instrument is basically a pole equipped with various metal ornaments (resembling a Chinese hat with a Turkish crescent above), a lot of jingling devices and numerous small bronze bells. The origin is unknown, although some sources talk about the Moors.

Wooden bells of Africa, Asia and South America are both decorative and signalling instruments. It seems that snakes, tigers and the Evil One disapprove of and dislike the ringing of bells.

Basic Bell Forms:

The Ball Bell:

This bell is rung by a loose little ball. For example: - the collar bells of a cat or dog, the row of bells on a horse harness and the Fool's cap of the Joker (the Gilles of Binche in Belgium).

Clapper Bell:

A bell with a swinging clapper, fixed on the inside, that strikes against the body by a shaking movement.

Claw Bell:

The edge shows a few bowed bars or claws. For example: - the bells of an elephant caparison.

Bodywork:

Bodywork means health therapies that involve manipulation of the body and its bioelectrical energy fields. Bowls can, by supply of energy, help with healing ideas, self-love and improving willpower. In this field we can consider: - Acupuncture, Acupressure, Alexander Technique, Ayurvedic Massage, Bio-Energetics, Chiropractic, Feldenkrais Technique, Massage, Metamorphosis Massage, Polarity, Rebirthing, Reflexology, Reichian Massage, Reiki, Rolfing (Structural Integration), Seiki-jutsu, Shiatsu, Speyertherapy, Therapeutic Touch and Touch for Health. Most bodywork takes into account the role of the mind and emotions in physical health, but a therapist cannot impose your sense of guilt! Bodywork involves a high level of (intuitive) awareness and prudence on the part of therapists.

Bowl Spirits:

Some people believe that spiritual entities are linked with the gentle, almost floating vibrations of singing bowls. In this vision spirits are the guardians of the bowls, who create a sacred space and force to link you with the divine. Attuning the bowls opens the veils between the material and the spiritual world, and calls up the spiritual guides, teachers, devas (personified elementary) and personal guardian angels.

These spiritual guides should give power to become a kind of priest of the bowls, but should also stimulate. Be careful in the application of magical and spiritual energy. 'Initiated' insiders suggest that spiritual servants should introduce themselves clearly and give certitude about possible negative forces.

We are talking here about 'other' dimensions, in which 'sacred' sounds, as a kind of catalyst, are responsible for intensified perceptions. In this context angels are mental forms who preserve the world from disintegration.

Spirituality, magic, healing and sounds are, in many cultures, interwoven with each other and with the harmonic energy of life. Like the human voice, instruments have a sacred reputation. Personal interaction with singing bowls for the inner world transforms energy and can help to liberate you from fear and frightening thoughts. Even in the New Age, the idea of spiritual guides makes many people feel uncomfortable. Fortunately, singing bowls, as ritual objects, can also become charged up with our own meanings, without the agreement of quantified angelic choirs or light creatures on rustling wings.

Ceramic Bowls:

Ceramicists and potters create artwork and pottery from clay. They talk about mouldable material, white porcelain solution, scratching the rims, engobes, mud flat, medium gravy, glazes (the icing on the cake) and fluctuations in bake-temperature. Native Indian Pottery is a brilliant result; see the Heard Museum in Phoenix, Arizona, USA. Certain ceramic bowls have delightful sounds and vibrations. Play on them with bamboo sticks or wands.

As a music and art reviewer, I know a lot of good Belgian ceramicists such as Octaaf Landuyt, José Vermeersch, Christien Dutoit, T'Jok Dessauvage, Jan Van De Kerckhove, Olivier Leloup, Achiel Pauwels, Carmen Dionyse, etc. Most of them also work in bronze. The paths of clay and metal alloys go through the same fire.

Chakras:

There is no accepted scientific evidence that chakras exist but, whatever we call these points, we can measure significant transformations in the energy potential in the areas where ancient healers indicated the energy centres. Many experts talk about the influence of sounds on human energy, via the chakras.

Chakras are believed to play a vital role in physical, emotional and mental health. They are shaped like multi-coloured petals or spoked wheels that whirl at various speeds as they process energy. A set of motives, attitudes and frames of mind are believed to belong to every chakra (meaning rotating knife).

The body's subtle energies are, under the influence of the chakras, converted into cellular, chemical and hormonal transformations. It is assumed that there are seven energy points, but it is food for thought that some people relate to the impact of a comet on Jupiter with the result that everyone disposes now of thirteen chakras. *Se non è vero, è ben trovato*! Let's hope that the result of this cosmic impact is already rectified, so that the seven chakras are in balance again with our familiar seven notes and colours.

1.- The basis (root) chakra	do or C	Red
2.- The sacrum (spleen) chakra	re or D	Orange
3.- The solar plexus chakra	mi or E	Yellow
4.- The heart chakra	fa or F	Green
5.- The throat chakra	so or G	Blue
6.- The third eye chakra	la or A	Indigo
7.- The crown chakra	ti or B	Violet

You haven't heard the last about the significance and the number of chakras for consciousness and healing. In the philosophy of traditional yoga, these seven chakras are like seven seals or subtle power strengths that inspire and control the whole physical body. This centre of activity is responsible for the receipt and transmission of the powerful energies of life. Chakra means wheel, disc or wheel on fire (Sanskrit). The chakras fit in an integral human view and holistic vision. In yoga, chakras are vortices that penetrate the body and the body's aura. A lot of spiritual philosophers (Leadbeater, Alice Bailey, Motoyama and others) pay much attention to these energy centres.

The discussion of contradictory meanings of transmission lines, kundalini, magnetic force, the existence of three (or more?) minor ethereal chakras and connections with endocrine glands or the seven Holy glands, is outside the scope of this book. To see the chakras as gates to different energy fields (colours, healing herbs, precious stones, gods and planetary influences) is one point. To create a kind of inquisition is another.

Singing bowls are refined tools to optimally gear the seven chakras. To let a bowl sing softly with a quiet rhythm gives support to your self-exploration. Play a bowl and make it sing. The most powerful means of playing a bowl is in a circular motion. The circle is a beautiful symbol, the lemniscate, that has no end or beginning. Look for a warm and low tune from your bowl. Repeat the playing and surrender to a harmonic inner awakening and spiritual transformation. As cosmic friends, sounds are the most subtle of the art forms with the greatest influence on our psychic centres and nervous system. Music is power. Music is life!

Suggestion:

Put a little bowl on every chakra. Put the seventh bowl on your surgery table at crown height. Strike them one by one. Change the tempo. Increase the speed, go slowly and nearly inaudibly. Move between soundless and warm singing. Let undertones and overtones ring out. Don't search for a system of notes or tonality; Himalayan bowls have a pure and absolute sound.

Chanting & Calming:

Chanting and singing by healers, shamans, medicine men and women have existed for centuries. Sounds are used in religious ceremonies, sacral hymns, colourful initiations and inspired rites; as guidance and support of healing, exorcism, invocations and sacral acts and proceedings. Every study of sound is a fascinating quest to discover spiritual traditions and primeval techniques. The application of sound as a calming or stimulating force descends from a rich and worldwide past: -

Ancient Egyptian papyrus mentions healing by sound. The Coptic Church is also the heiress of musical secrets originating in Egypt. In 324 B.C. Emperor Alexander recovered by lyre music.

The Old Testament relates that King Saul passed out of his depression after David played the harp. Opera singer Farinelli healed King Filips V in the 18th century with an aria. Pythagoras, the Greek philosopher, used for healing sounds the term 'harmonia'. Plato also recommended music as a remedy to ennoble spirit and emotions.

The Celtic Druids were responsible for the purity of their ritual and magical music. Celtic church choirs sang continuously in Glastonbury. Music and singing are the most important art forms in the rituals of the Holy Grail.

Mantras, Gospels and Gregorian chants are effective with one and the same sacral force. Religious music is liturgically connected and serves serenity in religious communities. The spiritual harmonies are relaxing and uplift the mind.

Rituals of the Church use the chasuble, chalice, monstrance, tabernacle, incense, burning glass and candles for ceremonial magic. Bells and gongs fulfil the same role.

Hindu yogis, Tibetan and Japanese monks, American Indians, Siberian Shamans, Celtic Druids, Mongolian Overtone singers, Australian Aboriginals and African magicians know the correct sounds to act on heartbeats, brain waves, respiration and perception.

Chinese Healing Music:

Chinese Yi-Ching music heals by the 'five-elements' theory. Old medical principles are linked with the energetic concepts of today. They provide revolutionary innovations in modern medical science. Alternative medicines are more than imaginary magic potions or placebos. The often-emotional dialogues between classical and alternative healers ebb away.

Church and Temple Bells:

Church and Temple Bells are bronze founded instruments with an alloy of 75% copper and 25% tin. The design shows a hollow and stump cone, bow outside on the bottom. A swinging clapper or hammer is fixed on the inside. Used as loud bell (church or temple), beat bell (tower clock) and play bell (carillon).

Most bronze church bells have a weight between ten and twenty tons. Exceptions are Asian bells of a two hundred ton weight.

The signalling function of church bells is similar to that of singing bowls, used to indicate the opening and closing of rituals, sessions and prayers. Bells have been present in church towers since the eighth century. Church bells indicate the beginning of Mass, benedictions and vespers. They are also used as fire alarms.

The keyboard carillon, which appeared in Flanders after 1500, consists of church bells controlled from a keyboard. It belongs to an old and rich tradition. Each note is played by the whole hand.

In Asia, bells are struck with a wooden beam. The 'kane' or 'densho' is a Japanese temple bell, also used in the off-stage music ensemble of the kabuki theatre, struck on the lower rim on the outside.

Circles:

The rim of a singing bowl is a circle that has no beginning or end. It is highly symbolic...George Harrison sings his touching song 'Circles' on the radio in my music room. I listen to his very poignant words about the soul that takes on a body. With each birth, we make indeed our date with life and death. Along this road the soul reincarnates. The ex-Beatle sings, "The show goes round and round in circles..." The circle, as humankind's most universal symbol and perfect shape in nature, can be found in the art and the spirituality of every culture. Spiritual scientists, philosophers and authors like Plato, Jacob Boehme, Carl Jung, Rudolf Steiner and Jill Purce, have devoted their genius and knowledge to exploring the meaning of the circle, one of man's central symbols, in dreams, art, religion and nature. A few examples:

Consecrated host in Christianity.
Circle of seasons.

Circle as time cycle.
Circle of Whirling Dervish Dancers.
Magical circle of witches.
Cosmic mandalas of the East.
Shaman mirrors.
Stonehenge.
Camp circles of Native American Indians.
North Rose Window in Chartres Cathedral.
Chinese Yin-Yang sign.
Symbol of oneness and eternity.
Halqahs, listeners in Islam mosques.
Paintings of Australian Aboriginals.
Double spirals carved by megalithic man.
Sun, moon and planets.
Astrologic diagrams.
Medicine wheels.
Crop circles.

Spiritual cultures like the Tibetan and Navajo (USA), on opposite sides of the earth, envision the circle as a most elegant rendering of peace, stability and unity.

Claims:

It cannot be denied that singing bowls are connected with the history of civilisations. No one person is their inventor or thief. Everyone can relax using various simple techniques, which points to the public character of this knowledge. An open mind and a considerable measure of scepticism are indispensable, for in this millennium time there is a lot of superstition and pseudo-science.

Cleaning:

Singing bowls that are to be used for healing and relaxation should be cleaned each time you use them. Clean and re-energise your singing bowls after every massage or relaxation. Clean them between sessions to seek the help of their inherent forces and energy.

Don't cover your bowls with grime, dirt or dust. Perspiring and sweaty feet can make your bowls smelly. Cleaning them will prevent discomfort on a future face massage. Guarantee hygiene. Relax and tune in to what your bowls are telling you.

The high energies of singing bowls can also be used to charge and clean precious stones and minerals, amulets and talismen or good-luck charms. Put the object(s) in a bowl and sound the bowl from time to time.

Colours:

Electro-crystal therapy use colours as a therapeutic remedy, which will, when united with sounds, direct research into new medical techniques.

Sit or lie down and close your eyes after playing a bowl. Let your breathing become deeper and slower. You can observe pulsating colours on the rhythm of overtones. Singing bowls can evoke colours that indicate infallibly the chakras where blockades of energy arise.

Connections:

"In nature, everything is connected and everything is alive."
                                                    G.I. Gurdjieff

Contra-Indications:

It is recommended that inexperienced people don't put crystal bowls or Himalayan bowls directly on the body of guests; they should only work at a safe distance. The power of bowls should not be underestimated. In case of any doubt, don't provide massage at all! Extra training by exchange of experience and evaluation is not a luxury.

Never put a bowl on the cicatrices after surgical treatment.

Never put a silica bowl on someone's head. They are fragile and dangerous!

Be careful with all kinds of bowls and gongs when treating children. Give them only a short massage.

Do not hit a bowl hard or play it too loudly. Aggressive vibrations after a thrombosis can provoke a new one, or a cerebral embolism.

Be very careful with heart patients (pacemaker!), brain damage, unsteadiness, impairment, epilepsy, cancer and psychiatric disorders or mental illness.

Be also very careful with pregnant women. Don't put bowls on breasts or stomach, except very cautiously as tender communication with the baby(s).

A preliminary talk is not redundant, it prevents vicissitudes with hyperventilation the extrication of old sadness and repressed frustrations. Provide a psychological safety net, certainly in public sessions. Some people change tack in a sound bath.

There are other circumstances in which it is best to be careful or advise against a sound massage: too high or too low blood pressure, burns, infections of the skin, risk of infection, traumatic fever, wounds, suspected lumps and complaints such as varicose veins, phlebitis and all fevers. Common sense and a consultation with a doctor go together.

Hyperactive children can be calmed by the soft sound of bowls, which means also that they can be over-stimulated by playing the bowls too loudly.

Give a sign to visually handicapped people when striking or beating loudly. It is not your intention to frighten them.

Don't drive a vehicle after a sound massage and don't work on machines that require concentration.

Creative Thinking:

In his masterpiece 'Janus, A summing up' (Ed. Hutchinson, London), Arthur Koestler wrote about verbal thinking that occupies our highest and lowest levels of mental hierarchy. This thinking can degenerate into rigid pedantry that puts a wall between our thinking and reality. Creativity sometimes starts where language ends, which means with a return to pre-verbal and apparently pre-rational levels of spiritual activity. These levels seem in some respect to be a dream, but maybe they are more related to the intermediate phases between sleep and wakefulness. Here Himalayan bowls are the right tools for developing and maintaining these breakthrough patterns. Logic is often an accurate instrument for problem solving, but sometimes we need 'creative thinking' to come within the reach of new opportunities and chances.

Singing bowls can be used during brainstorm-sessions and think tanks, which use creative thinking or creative thought. Through associations, sounds invite the discovery of clever and creative inventions, opportunities and new patterns. Strategic thinking is a powerful tool for guiding your mind into the future. To break patterns, sound helps to go beyond routine. When needed, creative thinking, expressive thinking and the sound of singing bowls can be interrelated to escape daily reality, routine and predictability.

Crotals:

Crotals are the traditional 'Cymbales Antiques'. There have been discoveries of Coptic crotals (400 B.C.) and much older antique cymbals. Similar instruments, the Zilia Massa, are still used in Greece. Crotals are small, round and thick bronze plates, made from CuSn20 bronze. They produce a pure and clear sound, with a perfect pitch. The chromatically tuned crotals are set up in a row. To facilitate playing chromatically tuned two octave sets, Paiste has developed a damper system. Crotals are struck, like a triangle, with an iron bar or with hard plastic mallets.

Crotals were often fixed to a forked piece of wood to form clappers in ancient Egypt. Debussy, who had a great interest in melodic and technical structures, used crotals in his composition 'Prélude à l'Après-Midi d'un Faune' in 1892.

Crystals:

'Crystal' descends from the Greek 'kristallos', which means 'clear ice' or 'frozen water'. Whoever says 'crystal' also says 'crystal ball'. A magical object and potent way to higher consciousness. Witchcraft and sorcery of Wisdom's Daughters, or romantic humbug? The facts are that crystal balls enjoy a lot of prestige and respect in different cultures. Crystal enjoys great fame and several forces in healing, divination and foretelling the future, balancing of emotions and energy and in a lot of secret and sacral rituals... Current study about crystals learns that: *Mother earth is a crystal.*

Crystals were a source of energy in the Great Pyramid of Giza. The keystone of this mysterious construction was also crystal.

Babylonians used crypto-crystalline to make magical and healing amulets.

The controversial English magician of the sixteenth century, John Dee, used a black crystal ball. A present from an angel?

Theophrastus, a disciple of Aristotle, mentioned crystals in 120 B.C. Plinius, the Roman, also wrote in his 'Naturalis Historia' about crystals.

Crystal-gazing is part of the Chinese ritual of ancestor adoration.

The Aboriginal medicine men (*coradjes*) often have a polished crystal on them as an aid to clairvoyance and for water detection. They keep this out of the view of others, especially women.

Medicine men in Central Africa bury crystal in sacred places to create and provoke rain.

A crystal bowl was found in the memorial grave of Merovingian King Childerik (A.D. 448 - 496). This is now in the Louvre.

The Romans used Rock crystal as fever therapy.

Mediaeval healers used to use pulverised rock crystal mixed with wine, against dysentery and colic.

Rock crystal, used as a light holder, was given by Native American Indians to their deceased.

Divers found a crystal bowl near the Bahamas; reason for speculation about a disappeared civilisation.

Roger Bacon (1214-1294) wrote in his book 'The history of Friar Bacon' about the manipulation of crystal balls.

Paraselsius (1493-1541) wrote in his manuscripts about crystal gazing.

During Shaman rituals, rock crystal is used for clear vision.

Mandalas are ritual diagrams, tools for Tantric meditation. One of these abstract mandalas is the Yantra, sometimes made of crystal.

Kirlian photography proves the existence of energy patterns of crystal.

Litho-therapy, healing with crystals and minerals, was taught until 1900 at universities in the Netherlands.

In the American Rhode Island Hospital in 1991 a modern scalpel was introduced, with 60,000 cycles per second produced by a vibrating crystal. This harmonic scalpel reduces the formation of scar tissue and prevents bleeding during operations.

Marcel Vogel, an IBM engineer, discovered that quartz crystal can be tuned into the frequency of water for medical use.

Scientists such as Igor Smirnoff and his wife, specialists in underwater deliveries, program water with crystal and teach babies a special swimming programme, which makes these children highly gifted.

Quartz crystals have many functions for treating different energies; amplification, convergence, pure conduction, modulation, input, age determination, transmission, reflection, refraction, stabilisation, transduction, re-balancing, transmutation, etc. Solar energy is also a possible application for crystals.

Crystal Skulls:

Enthusiastic bowl-lovers lay down between their singing bowls the most strange power objects: - I-Ching coins, pebbles, pieces of antler, horns, feathers, badger claws, snakeskin or Buddha sculptures of jade or crystal skulls... Are people joining (unconsciously) the great cultures?

In the Museum of Mankind in London is a precious crystal skull belonging to the pre-Columbian civilisation. This artefact was probably used in the initiation ceremonies of the Mayas. This archaeological showpiece was discovered in 1927 by Anna Hedges in the ruins of the Mayan town Lubaantun in British Honduras, now Belize. The weight of the skull is ten pounds; with our technical knowledge the skull can only be cut with a laser.

The skull shows accurate and anatomically correct details, but the back of the head is larger than the original hominids' skulls. A mystery that refers to Egypt? Or an extraterrestrial origin? Can we talk about a mind-machine or brain-machine with a mysterious energetic power? In any case, the unique skull is sometimes surrounded by an aura; images (not reflections) are visible in the skull, a strange smell is perceptible and, occasionally, rarefied bell-like sounds resound. Comparable to the sound of singing bowls?

F.R. 'Nick' Nocerino is a peace elder and founder of 'The Society of Crystal Skulls International' in 1945. At the Wolf Song IX Peace World Conference (August '98 in Holland) he talked about the 12+1 skulls created by 'Maya Time Masters' as the twelve characters of mankind, and as the holographic information centres for world-wide peace.

A big piece of rock crystal not only looks nice between a set of singing bowls, but it also intensifies the music experience. An ancient statement of great wisdom says, "When harmonic and pure music resounds near crystal, part of the spirit of the composer is captured in the crystal structure." It is not unusual, during a meditative listening to the bowls, to capture hidden messages in the music, but for rational people, all this stuff could be too soft.

Cuddly Stones:

Handy sized cuddly stones of Amethyst, Red Jasper, Rose Quartz, Rock Crystal or Tiger's Eye are mostly reasonably priced. Hold the cuddly stone in your hand with a positive mental attitude. To feel the power is easy: hold the crystal in your pocket or look to its sparkling glow. Charging a cuddly stone with a singing bowl is a fine experience.

Lay down the cuddly stone on a soft cushion (sand or silk).

Strike the rim of your bowl to bring over positive energy to the chosen stone.

Fix a cuddly stone on a mallet, this will be your magic wand.

Strike your bowls as an expression of your gratitude to the stones.

Cymbals:

Pairs of cymbals are used in Buddhist temple ceremonies and for exorcising of demons. It is said that when the sound of cymbals reaches its full intensity, the demon's brain is cleaved in two. Wadding probably protects the monks' ears, a hint for pop drummers? Cymbals belong, with castanets and tingshas, to the percussion family. They come in different sizes:

1. Big cymbals; one is held in each hand.
2. Big and small sized cymbals held on a tripod or the unipod of a drum.
3. Little finger cymbals as used by Turkish belly dancers. From *chengcheng* and *rinchik* in Bali, to castanets in the Spanish Flamenco.
4. Sizzle cymbals. Sizzles or rivets applied to your cymbales give the sonic illusion of a much longer sustain and a softer attack sound. There are no rules on whether it is better to use a light or heavy cymbal; both work well.

Appellation & Types:

The designation or name (splash, crash, etc.) of the cymbals depends on the factory, weight, format, cup form, etc.

Most music shops have a wide rang of brand names in stock. For example: Paiste, Zildjian, Meinl, Istanbul, UFIP and Sabian. Newcomers are: Grand Master, Turkish and Bosphorus.

The drum and percussion world cherishes its own jargon to talk about cymbals: crashes, swish, trashy, China splashes, hats, Turkish profiles, polite Chinese, thin crash, medium thin, signature crash, One of a Kind Custom Cymbal Shop Flatrides, etc.

Cymbals are, as self-sounding instruments with a simple structure, amongst the oldest idiophones in art music. The big dishes are still some of the most conspicuous devices in an orchestra. Several bronze pairs survive from classical Greece, Roma and mediaeval Europe.

Connoisseurs, sitting on exceptional kilims while tasting strong Turkish coffee, narrate a beautiful story about the cymbals... Long ago in the mysterious capital Constantinople (now Istanbul) lived the Turkish-Ottoman sultans with their elite troops, the famous Janitsar. It seems that in 1623 Avedis Zilçan, who was a member of this elite, invented the first cymbals to be used as a deafening deterrent. Although the descendants of Avedis Zilçan still produce the sublime Zildjian cymbals, they have tough luck because historical discoveries in China, Egypt, Tibet and Greece prove that the cymbals are much older...as early as 800 B.C.

Cymbals and plates of various shapes and sizes are very common in India; they are used in devotional singing and are all almost invariably made of bell metal, a particular variety, the Sapta dhatu (seven metals), of bronze. The instruments are called: Thali, Jhanj, Kansia, Chimta, etc.

Cymbal Cleaning:

Use the highly recommended 'Paiste Cymbal Cleaner'. This is the mildest cleaner you can get, especially designed for cymbals.

Never use harsh cleaners or buffing machines for cymbals, bowls, sound-plates or gongs. Buffing will change the sound. On black coating, use only a dry or damp cloth. Rub in the direction of the grooves. Use warm water and mild soap to remove dirt or stick marks.

Cymbal Storage & Transporting:

Some advice from Paiste:

Storage and transportation of your expensive cymbals is important to give them a long life.

Never rest them on their edge or against abrasive surfaces. Small nicks on the edge will cause cracks.

Pack your cymbals with soft materials. Cotton towel, soft felt or plastic sleeves, between them, will avoid scratches and damage.

Transport them in a bag or case; keep them separated with tissues or clothes.

Know who handles your cymbals, gongs and singing bowls.

Cymbals, Different Sizes:

Big cymbals, one is held in each hand. Big and small cymbals can be held on a tripod or the unipod of a drum.

Little finger cymbals are used by Turkish belly dancers. From 'chengcheng' and 'rinchik' in Bali to 'castanets' in the Spanish Flamenco. Finger cymbals produce a long, sparkling, silvery high, musical sound. They can be played as pairs with finger traps or suspended on a string, but also strung as a row to be played with sticks, mallets or triangle beaters.

Sizzle cymbals. Sizzles or rivets applied to your cymbals give the sonic illusion of a much longer sustained and a softer attack sound. There are no rules on whether it is better to use a light or heavy cymbal; both work well.

Cymbal Mounting:

For much more pleasure while playing your cymbals, choose proper stands and know how to mount your cymbals properly.

To prolong the life of your cymbals, check out your stands; be sure the felts are in good condition, with sleeves and washers on them.

The results of cymbals mounted on stands with bad felts, worn sleeves or oversized washers can be circular cuts on the underside of the bell, or a 'key hole' cut in the bell.

Make a final check before securing your sensitive cymbals with the wing nuts.

Cymbal Playing:

Choose the right cymbal for the situation.

Spend time, get familiar with your cymbals and their unique dynamic ranges.

In general it is best to angle your cymbals slightly towards you, to be able to hit them with a glancing blow.

Do not hit dead on with the cymbals mounted flat.

Do not hit with metal beaters.

Don't overplay your cymbals.

In general practice, the hollow sides of the cymbals are clashed, rim against rim, in a slanting and horizontal movement, against each other. Air resistance prevents a vertical strike.

Didgeridoo:

An unprecedented interest in 'World Music' and Australian aboriginal culture has helped to bring the visceral sound of the didgeridoo to our awareness. Free-floating tones, with a vast array of intricate rhythms, an unexpected echo and otherworldly tones, result when the didgeridoo is blown with circular breathing. The didgeridoo-player inhales through the nose while exhaling into the instrument through the mouth. Other names for the didgeridoo are: - Yidaki, Yaraki, Magu, Kanbi and Ihambilbing. This wooden trumpet or blowpipe is made from a eucalyptus tree branch hollowed out by termites, with a mouthpiece made of beeswax. The didgeridoo is a Folk instrument. The primal voice of 'mother earth' sings through the didgeridoo. Through this instrument the Australian aboriginals express their 'creation myths' and the wonders of nature. The continuous drone is very powerful. The didgeridoo is used in relaxation and dream accompaniment.

David Hudson, CD: Woolunda, Celestial Harmonies 13071-2.

Drumsticks, Mallets & Beaters:

The simplest principle concerning the mallets is: - "Better one bowl with ten beaters, than ten bowls with one beater." Make and construct your own drumsticks or mallets in order to gain a better understanding of the nature of woods, crystals and metals.

Drumsticks should be made of pliable hardwood, such as white oak, hickory, ash and elm. The best drumsticks are long and very slender.

Other names for a mallet or beater are stick, paddle, striker, wand, flog, cane, stake, baton, branch, stalk, staff, rod.

You should try a bow of a violin. Listen to the sounds in a rich harmonic coherence with long, continuous tones.

The beater, in wood or horn, of a shaman is wrapped with horse or elk fleece. Jingling little rings create extra sounds. Shamans throw their beaters in the air, and read their predictions by the way they drop down.

Beautiful and artistically carved wooden mallets, the finest you'll ever see, are for sale in large numbers in Kathmandu. Wood was abundant in Nepal. The Newari craftsmen are masters in engraving and carving wood with chisels, scrapers, drills and shavers. Graceful wooden mallets with detailed decoration, tantric symbols or mythical figures such as fishes, dragons and little squirrels are common. Unfortunately the Newari woodwork is at risk of becoming a dying art, vanishing as demand dwindles. Some tourists only buy small, cheap and crude pieces made by incompetent woodworkers. Now you can buy industrial plastic beaters and mallets in every country. Luckily, wooden mallets have not disappeared; they remain for sale in different sizes, forms and quality.

A 'Chalklin Mallet' of Paiste or a 'Cymbal Mallet' of Zildjian gives an excellent result on singing bowls. 'Percussion Plus', Ludlow Hill Road, Nottingham NG2 6HD, England, constructs reasonably priced beaters & mallets. Try their 'Slit Drum Beaters'!

Concerning drumsticks there are a wide rang of names: - Vic Futh, Vater, Pro-Mark, Regal, Kit Tools, Mainline Sticks, Supercussion, Zildjian, Paiste, etc. A newcomer is 'Pelwood Drumsticks', made by Hornbeam in the Pelisek stick-factory in Cestice, Czechoslovakia. Pelwood delivers a nicely priced and higher quality product.

Experience teaches that a little wooden hammer, equipped with self-adhesive felt, guarantees a beautiful purity of tone. Self-adhesive felt prevents dents in the shiny (polished?) wand of a singing bowl, or cracking in silica bowls.

Effects of Bowls:

Song and sound are still the ideal support for affirmations, prayers, congratulations, benedictions and other spiritual messages. Singing bowls are a stimulant in healing, a powerful aid to strengthen energy and advance harmonisation. The power of singing bowls is capable of very deep penetration, because every matter is made up of vibrations that work not only in a physical way. Liberation from suppressed emotions will provide liberation from sadness and sorrow. Awareness of the body is freedom to accept renewing energy. The healing power of singing bowls is needed when someone or something has become out of balance. When working with your bowls in relaxation or healing, you can invite the ancestors to bless you with their powerful wisdom and protection. It is, in this context that singing bowls replace or finish any medical treatment, without consultation, advice or judgement.

Animals can also enjoy treatment with singing bowls. A shaggy sausage dog needs different treatment to a strong Labrador. Some people treat even their houseplants with the energy of singing bowls.

He who closes his eyes, after playing a bowl, can observe pulsating colours on the rhythm of overtones. The sound of bowls can bring you to a state of trance, in which mystical and magical qualities gain power. There is obviously a matter of a meditative level of consciousness. Singing bowls can evoke colours that indicate the infallible chakras, where blockades of energy arise.

Encircling:

Encircle the bowls, play them by running the wand along the edge. The friction between wand (male) and bowl (female) creates an undulating vibration, a sound that emanates from the so-called womb of the bowl. This circular motion basically builds up a singing drone by running a piece of wood around the rim of a bowl. This circular playing provides the name 'Singing' bowls. The sound is really circling around to clean up the environment with new energy and higher creativity. The sound circles to restore the balance around and through your-self. The circle of the spirit?

Rubbing backwards and forwards in one place on the rim also provides the singing tone. An annoying rasp can be prevented by adjustment of pressure and encircling or with a strip of plastic on the wand.

Leather-bound wands and vegetarians are not compatible. Usually encircling a singing bowl clockwise provides positive energy; invokes, releases and draws the tones into the body.

Start a relaxation or meditation session with a counter-clockwise rotation to ground yourself, to receive inner energy, to stimulate power and to draw out negative patterns of mind and body. Counter-clockwise rotation draws out negativity.

Energetic Set:

It is good to open the force in your hands before a sound massage. Make, in silence, a stretching movement with your arms. Turn a palm of the hand to the earth, and one to the sky. Close your eyes. Make a fist at the same time with both hands twenty times. Change the direction of your palms and make a fist twenty times again. Open your hands and bring them with stretched fingers slowly and calmly to each other at breast height. You will feel a resistance, at about ten centimetres, between both hands. This resistance feels like a rubbery ball full of tingling energy. You can also play an imaginary piano in the air... Touch first slowly and cautiously, then fast and energetically, the invisible keys. Rub your hands. Bring both hands relaxed to each other. Use the force of your imagination to visualise the ball of energy. To round off, give one quiet roll on a tambourine, darabuka, djembé or Shaman hand drum. Feel how the rhythm gives power to your fingers and how a warm tingling radiates from your hands.

It's good to use Chinese Meridian Ball's (Shou-xing) to keep your hands in an excellent condition. These metal balls grade up your co-ordination and your manual skill.

Ethical Code:

It is not suggested that singing bowls replace or finish any medical treatment. To play doctor is irresponsible and even criminal. Some people link bowls with organs. They talk about a liver bowl, a heart bowl, a stomach bowl, etc. The facts speak for themselves, in this particular use medical knowledge is indispensable. Please, use the bowls for relaxation, but don't practice medicine! Only doctors have the right to diagnose and prescribe medications.

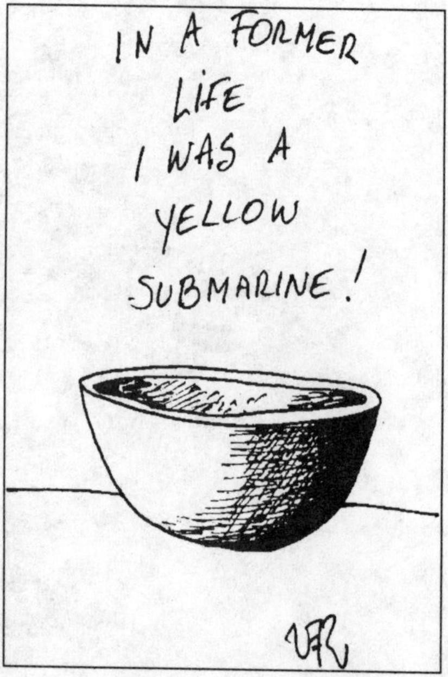
IN A FORMER LIFE I WAS A YELLOW SUBMARINE!

Flowerpots:

Amateurs of original sounds should try playing flowerpots. Listen to the following recommendable CD's of Stephan Micus. He is a master on flowerpots, unusual as melodious and harmonious instruments. This German musician, living in Mallorca, brings powerful and emotive compositions. Not only on flowerpots, but also on nay, shakuhachi, Bavarian zithers, hammered dulcimers, sattar, acoustic guitars, sarangi, suling, etc. Stephan Micus is really one of my favourites, with a great impact on my life. He is renowned for creating music that bridges cultures and influences... and what a voice! He performs solo with meditative, lyrical and mystifying compositions; New Acoustic Music, with a minimum of ornamentation and a lot of creativity. His music feels like it's being created in the moment. The unusual sensitivity of this outstanding musician is an inspiration for every bowl-lover.

This is timeless music.

CD: **Behind Eleven Deserts**
Intuition Records INT 3042-2
CD: **Wings over Water**
ECM Records, 831058-2

CD: **Athos**
ECM Records, 523292-2
CD: **Twilight Fields**
ECM Records, 835-085-2.

Flute:

That the creation of the first flute might have been suggested
to man by the wind whistling through holes in bamboo, is an old
belief. More likely seems the common act of whistling. Flutes
have strong socio-religious associations. For example, the use
of the flute in sacred, ceremonial and ritual music of the indigenous North Americans, can be traced back at least 2500 years
through oral traditions and ancient carvings. Flutes have a strong
phallic significance and special functions in certain sexual rites.
In some primitive clans, if a woman saw a flute she was killed!
Luckily the flute became a symbol of the divine, erotic trans-
formed into esoteric. Extremely beautiful moments of interplay
between flute and bowls are possible. Among the great com-
poser-performers, R. Carlos found a role for the Native American flute in beautiful multi-cultural settings. The flute is an
aërophone instrument with a mouthpiece.

In ancient Etruscan paintings we can see the first side-blown
flutes. Flutes are made of various materials as: bamboo, bone,
clay, copper, horn, ivory, reed, silver, wood, etc.

Aristotle placed great power in flute music to rouse emotions
and provide catharsis. The Tibetan Kangling is carved of a
human thighbone. The sound banishes the demons

When played in a pure style, the Japanese Shakuhachi, the
Bolivian Ujusini, the Slovakian overtone-flute or Fujara and the

Nguru of the Maori-people sing with the same magical, fascinating power of the marvellous singing bowls.

Focused use of Sounds:

You can find singing bowls on marked places and in small shops, between masks of beauties and beasts. I saw little bowls mistreated as ashtrays and big bowls used as buckets for dirty rags. Personally I heard good, bad and ugly-sounding bowls. The good-sounding bowls are a major contribution to a higher consciousness.

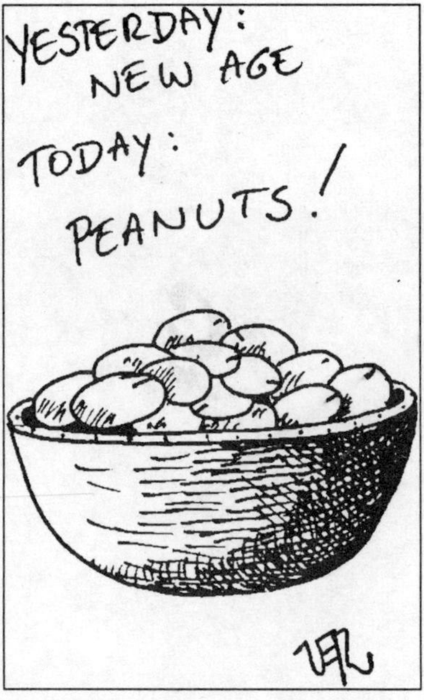
YESTERDAY:
NEW AGE
TODAY:
PEANUTS!

Ghatam:

Heard in Karnatak music concerts. The ghatam is similar to the noot, made of special clay, uniformly fired. The player sits on the floor, his shirt open; the mouth of the pot is held close to the stomach and is not beaten on the mouth. By manipulating the abdomen, the player can elicit various sounds and volumes. The gourd of the Brazilian berimbau and the double beat-bell of Ghana are used in the same way.

Glass Bowls/Glass Harmonica:

From the late Middle Ages there are pictures of musical glasses, built in different sizes and sometimes tuned by water filled to different levels. They are struck by a mallet or by rubbing the edge with a dampened finger. In 1762 Benjamin Franklin caused the glasses to revolve by means of a treadle. The Glass Harmonica was born.

The sound of the singing bowl is indeed comparable with the high-pitched sound of a crystal wineglass, rubbed by a dampened finger. Gluck, the eighteenth century opera composer, earned much honour in 1746 with his concerto for 26 singing glasses. Mozart and Beethoven composed for the glass harmonica. Baschet (Paris) even developed a glass trombone.

Now, Danny Becher (Holland) plays glass bowls, which not only have their own sounds, but also blend exquisitely with Himalayan bowls. The sound compositions are formed by two blue glass bowls.

Becher, Danny   CD: In Resonance. Oreade, Holland ORP 59142.

Gongs:

Gongs, also known by the name tam-tam, are East-Asiatic, bronze percussion instruments, created entirely by hand. They are related to single cymbals, hung up vertical or horizontally, with a raised size, on a stand. Usually a gong has a diameter of 50-150 cm (20-60 inches). The surface is flat or slightly rounded, and the outer edge is bent backwards. They originate from the Han Dynasty (200 BC) in China. The first gongs were flat; later on, a cup was added (Java).

A gong is struck from the front side with a stick, wrapped in felt or covered by fur. The sound goes from a clear note cushioned softly by complimentary harmonics to a dark, rumbling and thundering resonant voice. Composers like the overwhelming 'fortissimo' in the climaxes of their compositions, see for example the Video ' Pink Floyd at Pompeii' (RM Productions PPS-2010).

In Japan the rather solid 'Shoko' is a gong that produces a dry high-pitched sound when struck on its concave back.

Gongs have also applications beyond music, in recreation, therapy, performance art, religion, relaxation and meditation. A few well-trained therapists use large-sized gongs for kidney massage.

A Few Gongs:

Shan-trom and Kungh-Zee (Myanmar, ex-Burma).
Yun Lo of Yun Ngao (China).
Tam âm la (Vietnam).
Gamelan (Indonesia & Java).
Kenong, Raffles-Gamelan, Gong and Bonang (Java).
Symphonic Gongs (Paiste), with a harmonic and universal sound structure.
Tuned Gongs (Paiste), feature a boss to produce a specific note.
Sound Creation Gongs (Paiste).

Each gong has its own extraordinary and particular sound character. Their impressive, charismatic sound embodies a wealth of archetypal emotional sensations and truths. These gongs with a wide range of harmonics and frequencies are favoured for healing sessions and in demand for relaxation.

Planet Gongs (Paiste) resemble Symphonic Gongs in character, but feature a strong fundamental note tuned to represent a natural harmonic series based on the orbital properties of the Sun, the Earth, the Moon and the other planets.

Deco Gongs are well known with a small decorated element, like the inside of a Chinese take-away restaurant. The fundamental note of every gong is balanced with the instrument's complex overtones. Featuring some of the largest gongs on earth.

GONG, CD: Jens Zygar (Star Sounds Orchestra):

Planets	Fønix Musik FMF CD 1051
Gongs	Fønix Musik FMF CD1053
Klangraüme	Fønix Musik FMF CD 1063

Growing Pains:

The most difficult part of healing is not the techniques but the personal growing pains. Look out for healers, spiritual teachers and gurus who do not live as they preach. Examine yourself and question when using advanced technique, if you are spiritually matured. The simple and universal techniques mentioned in this book do not make a bowl healer of you, neither do they ask for an argument about quantum physics, energy expansion or the divergent aspects of the higher self. They are only a first acquaintance to remind you that you are not practising medicine.

Handling:

Working with bowls is a companionship and a kind of home study. The results always conform to your efforts and commitment. Only using the singing bowls now and then can make it difficult to see through the real nature of the bowls. Regular practise is necessary. Gain knowledge and experience via a positive mental attitude and by observing consciousness. Most people are capable of localising energetic blockades in their body. Placing a bowl in a sensitive area will prove quickly how much sounds work into negative thinking patterns, hidden emotions and repressed sadness.

Hearing:

Hearing is the first sense that develops in the secret sea of a safe mother's lap. Research at the British Universities of Keele and Bath proves that unborn babies can hear and memorise sounds after the first twenty weeks during the pregnancy, or about one month earlier than previously assumed. Results of investigations demonstrate that not only the cortex but also the lower part of the brain is responsible for the development of the memory, perception and hearing. It is proved that during the process of dying, the hearing is the last active sense. Sounds and hearing are brilliant, linked wonders.

Himalayan Singing Bowls:

The introduction of singing bowls to the West started in the late sixties. The flower power of the hippie-movement in California discovered Asia with a 'love and peace' message and of course a few dollars! The sitar became 'hip'. Ravi Shankar, now probably the best-known Indian musician known for his experimental interests, became a hero. Even the famous and influential Beatles ended at the Maharishi's shoeless feet in Rishikesh, India. Since then the 'fashionably' popular singing bowls have been imported from Nepal and India (Assam, Bengal and Orissa). They are described as Tibetan meditation gongs, secret Shaman or religious music-instruments, therapeutic or curative bowls, tableware for pregnant women or as ritual attributes of Bön-Pö monasteries. Astrology is also connected with the singing bowls. Their probable age is difficult to discover.

Hospice Care:

Singing Bowls are also very powerful in Hospice Care (Terminal Care). Certainly in nursing and home care, bowls can be used, when tapped softly to suppress pain, to reduce fear and to prevent vigilance. Through my own experience I have learned that dying people have more comfortable hours after a bowl session. Dying is still connected with spiritual pain. Send, together with the sound vibrations of your bowl(s), love to the dying person. This requires mental stability. Views about meaningful interaction with fear, dying and psycho-social assistance are necessary. The spiritual needs of a terminal person are, besides company, an affectionate and warm presence. It is a matter of great importance to accept that it is dangerous and naive to suppose that peace, mildness and dignity can come out of the singing bowls, just like that. Most of the time, dying is surrounded by desperately tragic and hopeless sadness. Spiritual aid, care for a social frame and warm solidarity are the real support. In these circumstances, experiments with bowls are excluded!

Looking back in tenderness... Dad nods assenting. My small singing bowl sings carefully on his heart chakra. Dad closes his eyes and pinches my hand. Velvet sounds vibrate inside, "Let everything go. Go now..." Dad smiles, "It will not take long." Young sunlight caresses his face. Hardly two hours later, Dad surrenders to the biggest secret. Mum dies two days later. My singing bowls are singing differently now... going beyond the daily sounds. Can you hear the heartbeat of dad and mum in the good vibrations?

Human Body:

It is not foolish to assume that the human body is the first idiophonic instrument. Did you never clap your hands and stamp your feet or slap thighs and hips to accompany music and dances? The next step is easy to imagine: the use of stones, wood and metals to make louder music. And the beat goes on...

Hurdy Gurdy:

The hurdy-gurdy is the only instrument to be started by the turning of a wheel, related to a never-ending bow. It originated in the 12th and 13[th]centuries. This strange, mysterious instrument is reported, like Singing Bowls, to have connections with the imaginary, magic and received ideas.

The Bowls also stimulate the imagination and invite you to start a search operation to discover new sounds and a particular colour of sounds. Maybe you should design and develop your own instruments? Rub and polish, let buzz and ring. Welcome flutes and aërophonic instruments. Buy yourself a unique Swedish Nyckelharpa or a Korean Kayakeum citer... Beat the music bowls and study the chordophones as sitars and harps in relationship with your singing bowls.

Idiophonic Instruments:

It is not unreasonable to assume that idiophonic (ghana vadya) instruments are the oldest musical instruments used by mankind. The human body involves all the rhythmic acts and primeval movements. Hands are clapped, thighs and hips struck with hands to accompany dance, music and ceremonies. Singing bowls are part of the idiophonic instruments.

Incense:

A smudge stick is a bunch, bound together with a cotton string, of sage, thyme and rosemary. Smouldering gives a powerful and purifying smell. Put out with sand.

A Himalayan bowl with an inferior sound can be used as a mortar to pulverise and mix herbs or incense. Such a bowl, filled with sand, is also an excellent holder for joss sticks.

Introduction:

If there is any negative reaction or rejection, stop the introduction. Let your guests or receiver(s) sit down in a comfortable position. Tap a big bowl and let the receivers feel the vibrations by their fingertips. Play the bowl in front of your guest(s). Move from foot to head and upside down. Move from front to back, from back to front. Surround the body for a while with the sound of your bowl.

Let your guest (s) lay down. Play several bowls and let the sound that delights the ear, caress your guest(s). Silence inbetween is also flattering. A walk around with a buzzing Himalayan bowl amongst an interested audience provides a distinctive and cosy ambience. Perhaps you should give your audience more time to discover their own suitable singing bowl. Some people need more time to be deeply affected by the peculiar sound of singing bowls.

Even today, I am still learning about the mysterious and most rewarding bowls. I hope that it will always be like this. No one is master the first day. Andrés Segovia, the famous classical Spanish guitarist, once said: " It is better to be a pupil of art at 90, than a master at 14!"

Irritation:

It's my sincere conviction that what is experienced as disagreeable or offensive should be taken seriously. There is no doubt; in case of irritation, feeling of sickness or pain, every treatment with singing bowls should be terminated. Your technique will only improve by permanent evaluation.

Isbin, Gilbert:

A Belgian self-taught guitarist, born in Knokke on 29th May 1953. Already at an early age he was inspired by European improvised music and modern jazz, especially the minimalist approach of Paul Bley, Bill Evans and Leo Brouwer. As a mature and impassioned artist, Gilbert created his own style, especially characterised by strong melodies and subtle and rich guitar playing. His compositions are evocative and original, set in delicate, minimalist arrangements with a scope that embraces polyrhythm, collage and free jazz. With this excellent friend and guitarist, I was very happy to produce the CD 'Twins' in 1999. 'Eurock on line' wrote about this CD:

"It has been some time since I have heard new material by Belgian guitarist Gilbert Isbin (remember the beautiful and pristine work 'Pure'?). The good news is that 'Twins' is even better. A collaborative work with percussionist Geert Verbeke, the music is a mystical fusion of classical guitar, and prepared guitar soundscapes, complemented beautifully by a variety of exotic percussive textures (a/o. singing bowls, piano, cymbals and gongs) and effects. The sound is simple, spatial and organic with the emphasis shifting from a traditional guitar sound to experimental passages with ease. Highly recommended."

Information: http://users.pandora.be/gilbert.isbin

Islamic Bowls:

Prof. Remke Kruk, University of Leiden, Holland, mentions that Islam also uses a kind of bowls. Not only bowls with written messages of the Koran on the inside, but also magical bowls filled with water. The water in these so-called 'frightening bowls' is stirred with a kind of key with an Ankh-symbol. Drinking the water disperses the fear. The oriental heroic story about Sayf Ibn Dhî Yazan talks about a magical bowl, the tâsa, filled with water. When this powerful water was sprinkled on Sayf and his companions, they were paralysed.

Jala Tarang:

Perhaps the Indian 'Jala Tarang' is the missing link to discover the roots of the bowls... 'Jala' means water, 'Tarang' means wave. It consists of a water xylophone, with a number of little porcelain bowls of different sizes. The number depends on the notes to be played. The variety in height, width and thickness determines the pitch of these earthenware bowls. Into each bowl is poured a prescribed amount of water to adjust the pitch to the required sound. Tuned with water they offer a beautiful euphony. The set-up of the water-filled bowls is a circle, with the player in the centre. A similar set-up is used by gong players in Thailand and Myanmar (Ex-Burma). Usually the melody is struck on the rims of the pottery with two small bamboo sticks, but sometimes the Jala Tarang is played with wet fingers. It is even said that the warrior Alexander, on his way back to Macedonia from India, took with him some Jala Tarang players. It seems that Vatsyayana's Kamasutra speaks of an 'Udaka Vadya' or 'water instrument'... the Jala Tarang?

The folk varieties of this instrument are made of clay or metal under the names *matki*, *gagri* and *noot*.

Japanese Bowls:

Metal bowls from Japan, with a diameter of two inches are connected with Zen Buddhism and with the divine germinate power of the respectable Shinto-religion (the way of Kami or gods who inspire the landscape). Purchasing these rare Japanese bowls is a question of time, patience and a lot of money.

The Japanese Dobachi or Keisu, a big bowl (80 cm high), is decorated with dragons and family crests. It always rests on an undercarriage or on a cushion, which does not dampen the sound. This cushion prevents the bowl from toppling over when struck. Such a bowl has a strong resonance of a few minutes.

Thailand, Korea and Myanmar (Burma) are in a limited way also familiar with bowls (and gongs). They are linked to Buddhist rituals and ceremonies. Unfortunately most of these bowls are fake or cheap replicas with an expensive price tag.

Jew's Harp:

A metal frame, neither Jewish nor a harp, placed against the mouth. The player flicks a metal tongue with his finger. By altering his mouth position, a harmonic sound will be heard. The sound merges easily with singing bowls.

Kathmandu:

During August 1999, thanks to my wife Jenny, I visited the Kathmandu Valley in Nepal for an instructive trip. Thank you, no trekking for me! I prefer the masterpieces of art produced in the three mediaeval city capitals: Kathmandu, Patan and Bhaktapur. They are almost entirely religious in character. The marvellous legacy is all inspired by the gods. The great shrines of Swayambhunath, Pashuputinath and Bhaktapur are inspiring. I admire the genius of the Newari people. Over the centuries the Newari artists have produced a wealth of superb masterpieces such as sculptures, statues, monuments, paintings and ritual artefacts.

If you travel to mysterious Nepal, then you will certainly find reasonably priced (new) Himalayan bowls. In Kathmandu you can search in the environs of Ganga Path, the mediaeval city with Durbar Square, and in the new city with Durbar Marg forming the central axis. Try also the countless little shops for the tourist trade in the tiny side streets and crumbling courtyards of Thamel. Investigate different qualities and prices. Don't shop in luxury hotels; it is better to check out the small craft shops. Beautiful ritual objects and 'antiques' are for sale around the great stupa of Boudhanath, five miles from Kathmandu;

also in Patan above the Bagmati River and in Bhaktapur, also known as Bhadgaon. Take time and patience to look around. Be careful... the cat knows whose beard she licks!

Classic Nepali metalwork, which ranks among the world's finest, is a caste occupation passed on from father to son. Most artists saw the first light of the day into the highly traditional and formalised profession. Skilled metalworkers produce ritual accessories like bells and bowls in gilded copper and bronze, with a high proportion of copper giving a ruddy glow. Today a few master metalworkers remain; they preserve the ancient technique of 'cire perdue' or the 'lost wax' process of casting. Modern craftsmen, who rarely match the skill of the old ones, have shifted to brass, a less expensive alloy of copper and zinc, to produce more mundane portable pieces, such as small carved bowls, for tourists.

Kathmandu's Durbar Square is a wide area, with beautiful temples and monuments, swarming cycle rickshaws, fluttering prayer flags, girls in their ceremonial finery, street traders, temples with detailed woodwork and woodcarvings, hooting cars, roaring motorbikes, three-wheelers and rich sadhus begging dollars from the tourists.

Now, traders appear wherever tourists stray, with various folk objects as good purchases. Among them are the khukris, the national knife, and the saranghi, a small four-stringed viola. Also for sale are incense burners, 'Free Tibet' cotton shirts, wool jackets, little oil lamps, ennobled prayer wheels, silver-plated jewellery, hand-made paper, papier-mâché dance masks, filigree brass animals and all kinds of heavy copper or brass pots, jugs, jars. One also finds copper or bronze statuettes of various

Hindu deities and Buddhas of all sizes. And, of course, the famous singing bowls with a lot of highly imaginative information.

Kathmandu valley is a real treasure trove for unwary tourists. Consider 'antique' bowls, unless otherwise certified by specialists, to have been made a few days before. Keep in mind the value of the rupee and bargain to get a good price. Be ruthless with the street vendors of singing bowls, who ask for and try to get ridiculous prices for their generally trashy bowls.

Kinds of Bowls:

You can make your choice;

Himalayan singing bowls
Japanese singing bowls
Ceramic bowls
Glass bowls
Silica bowls (USA).

Origin, alloy and design determine the timbre of singing bowls. Sound vibrations work instinctively. Contact with bowls supplies illumination. Maybe you will discover the musician in yourself. Don't be surprised.

Huge number and thickness of all sizes, and, of course, the Japan single layer is much more highly integrative in manufacture.

Equipment under a single incise towards the ... Quartz ... in ... more ... ... so the exhibits to have been made a few days before. Keep in mind the value of the exhibits and bargain to get a good price. Be fearless with this art. Vendors of items in boxes who ask for a out ... to get the right price for their generally trashy bowls.

Kinds of boats

You can make your own shapes:

Flat glass drying boats
Japanese quartz bowls
ceramic boats
Clay boats
Silica boats (USA)

Once in a blue and each item a time machine of Ming-ly bowls. Second summer work in situ ... very ... Contact wild bowls are plus millimeters. Maybe ... you will discover the most Ming ... self. Don't be surprised.

Listening:

Singing bowls offers the perfect music for giving or receiving a massage. The gentle music and enchanted sound of singing bowls follows the movements of the masseur, creating an ideal ambience for massage. When there is no one around to supply a massage, just listen to a CD with singing bowls, sail away on sweet dreams and find the treasure of pure relaxation... Listening to the captivating tonal variety of the singing bowls is considered to stabilise body, soul and mind, which react to sound vibrations. You can use singing bowls instead of a cup of coffee to help you digest lunch, to help you sleep and to help you recover from illness. Be sure to listen for at least ten minutes while focusing only on the soft sound of singing bowls. Listen to the bowls, instead of having two whiskies after an overloaded working week.

Maintenance:

It is clear that singing bowls, like other instruments, need maintenance and loving attention. The treatment, however, varies according to circumstances.

Usually metal bowls have a golden glow, sometimes a matt grey glow, dependent on the alloy. Some bowls have a dim black lacquer on the outside. Removing this can change the timbre of the sound.

The using of aggressive means as hydrochloric acid or other corrosive products is disastrous for the bowls. Sandpaper and steel wool are taboo! It is still questionable whether singing bowls need to be cleaned up to a mirror finish. Ceramic and silica bowls cannot bear chemical treatments.

Temperature has no influence on the sound of Himalayan bowls. Fluctuations in temperature can be the cause of condensation on the inner side of crystal bowls, which means that these bowls can no longer be struck with a rubber wand. A damp cloth is the remedy for this evil.

For cleaning use distilled water with 10% solution of biodegradable detergent. Water is a universal and living cleaner. Cleaning your bowls in the flow of the sea or a river is of course an obvious way. You can also clean with warm soapy water. Dry carefully after cleaning, or put your bowl in the sunlight. Place your bowls outside in the sunlight for 24 to 48 hours. At the time of full moon, the charging is much more effective. Use nature's high energies to re-energise and to clean all your singing bowls, bells and gongs.

Wands or mallets also merit careful treatment. Wrap them in cloth (silk, wool or cotton) or put them in a protective cover.

Herbs give substantial power for protection and purifying. Lighting candles, for purification, is also powerful.

Exposure to incense of jasmine, myrrh, olibanum, bergamot, rosemary, etc. neutralises the potential negative energy of bowls and other instruments. For preference, use granular incense. Strew the incense sparingly on smouldering charcoal in a censer. The granules are more difficult to use than the handy joss sticks, but the smell and the power are much better. Let the odour of sanctity be closely connected with the soundscapes.

Cleaning with visualisations also takes effect; visualise how a stream of positive energy cleans up your singing bowls. If bowls are used regularly, the playing itself is a charge and cleaning.

Magical Storytelling:

Magical storytelling is one of the treasures of mankind. Myths, fairy tales, old legends, epic, fables, parables, poetry or ballads express the symbolic and spiritual language of different cultures. Used by ancient mystics and bards to open perception and emotions, storytelling can also guide meditation, establish contacts and evoke enlightenment. A storyteller can also help translate psychic reality into images, develop magical states and the power of higher consciousness. Storytelling uses dynamic musical effects in, for example, puppet theatre, relaxation and shamanism. Magical storytelling is more powerful with music and creative tones. Singing bowls, tingshas, gongs and cymbals are very effective tools for this process. Do you write your own fairy tales? Try to create your own story about singing bowls.

Look for symbols and images in following story. Explore and expand... Be Alwana. Be Erbou. Place yourself in their characters and explore the whole story. Take your time to meditate on this important subject of transformation through music and words. Write your own fairy tales.

Alwana:

Dedicated to Ted Andrews-

On the coast of Ranapour in faraway Circadia lived Alwana. Her simplicity was that of a pebble in a murmuring mountain brook. She knew the secrets of flowers and balm, the magic of candles and incense. The languages of frogs, crickets and bees were also known to her. Sunlight caressed the seven fertile slopes around Ranapour. Red beech, oak, lime, spruce and sacred ash contained the essence of the universe.

Alwana touched her Singing Bowls made from seven metals to calm her mind, balance her body and to induce trance conditions for vision quests. The sacred sounds were unified with the spirit of the soothing landscape. Alwana healed with medicinal herbs, seaweed, mosses and the wave patterns of her

Sacred Bowls. In her proximity, amethyst, topaz and rock-crystal sparkled with an unknown glow. She lived richly in her modesty, modestly in her richness. She knew how to handle fire and water as healing powers. As if devoted Alwana read the signs in the whorls of shells and corals. Where butterflies fluttered as flying blossoms, she meditated in lucid consciousness. In the sandy earth she recognised the powers that also live in the abundance of water, clouds and fire. Alwana continued to draw strength from loving attention. With an inner power she experienced the peacefulness of the lagoons, felt intensely how with its tranquil waves the sea infiltrated dolphins and turtles with lucid consciousness.

Alwana saw life itself in the flood mark. She knew about the cycle of the seasons which ceaselessly breathes new life into itself, to bring slumbering seeds to germination. Alwana understood that water must splatter and tumble down in its own depth in order to become a smooth mirror. While the sea was telling the faraway horizon fairy tales, Alwana placidly observed the waves without passing judgement on low tide or high tide. In tender attention Alwana was liberated of fear. Her loving was free from the pressure of the spirit with its eternal desires. Alwana's modest singing about pomegranate, yellow mélilot or quince always sounded as clear as ever. Even when singing that fishes and waterlilies are understood only by the one who dares swim upstream.

Then Erbou the date merchant would sullenly stare out in front of him. Ripe rice paddies were the answer to the tender fusion of water and earth. Alwana understood, but remained modest as a grain of sand in the deepest of seas. For the envious Erbou this was torment. Frequently his hand clawed for the hilt of his lethal dagger. Envy could not harm Alwana. Quietly she mixed scented oils of daffodil, hyacinth and benzoic as a sacrifice to inner peace, scattered a mixture of myrrh, saffron and rosehip on smouldering charcoal. A hummingbird followed the fragrant wreaths of smoke. Erbou cursed this little miracle. Ranapour offered a peaceful sight. Fragrances of exotic fruits blended with the sweet aroma of spices. Cinnamon, clove and jasmine were an offering. Furiously, Erbou reached for his whip. Alwana remained unmoved. The whip changed into a blooming twig. Alarmed, Erbou shrank back into the shadows of the under-growth. His voice shaking, he exclaimed: "From now on I will combat your witchcraft, break your strength!" Alwana, know-ing that loving deeds do not wrinkle the pond of the heart, only smiled...

His feverish eyes filled with envy, Erbou looked closely at the lovely Alwana. She looked at him and said: "Lord, your wishes will come true, even if the nightingale's chant has to die!" A peel of thunder reverberated between the vineyards and the gnarled olives. For weeks the date merchant Erbou sent no news. Driven by greed, he finally showed up at Ranapour's marketplace. With a drawling voice he begged Alwana to un-veil the future for him from the hazes of time. Courteously Alwana pointed out the magnificent hills surrounding Ranapour. "Lord, behold how the slope's flanks undulate fruitfully in the sunlight. When the white amaranth in the desert will bloom, your fields will bear fruit. Abundance will be your season's yields."

Then what Alwana foretold came true. Erbou gained unknown riches and esteem. His treasures glittered like the scales of sunfishes. Sparkling precious stones were as numerous as the bunches on the vines' branches. Fabulous riches accumulated. The roll of drums reverberated, the kettledrums rumbled. The inhabitants of Ranapour assembled to catch but one glance of the former date merchant. Haughtily Erbou rode past them. Ranapour wrapped itself up in dispirited silence. Even the birds kept quiet... Ranapour's marketplace smelled of incense and honey. Disdainfully, Erbou sniffed the air and sneered: "As clairvoyant you knew what was going tot happen, didn't you? Be off! Never again let your shadow soil my path." Alwana left. A rainbow coloured the horizon.

Finally Erbou lived the life of a recluse in a sombre citadel. Barbarian warriors kept watch with ferocious dogs, for diamonds and rubies filled the trunks and jars in Erbou's treasure-cellars. Despite his immense richness, Erbou was a bitter man. Around him, he saw only gossip, intriguing and flattery. His bitterness grew. Yet once in a while there was a stroke of melancholy, when Erbou remembered the simplicity of the olden days. During those vulnerable moments, Erbou sent for wine to seek comfort and oblivion in intoxication. Bindweed bloomed, bear's breech grew, Turkish turtledoves cooed. Flowers reached for the light in the countless dewdrops.

A Singing Bowl sounded three times. Alwana's arrival was announced to Erbou by a servant. Despise and deep disgust filled the heart of the cruel sovereign. With a crash the draw-bridge came down. Two grim guards brought Alwana up. Her noble attitude radiated strength. Erbou stared at her, overpowered by fear. Suddenly he threw a golden slumber at her, screaming: "I will kill you like a snake!" Grinning, Erbou signalled his guards, grabbed a smoking torch from a ring in the wall, and dragged Alwana down the spiral stairs. With a hissing sound the candles extinguished. A smell of decay rose. Erbou's laughter drowned the chains' clank. A cold wind roared. In the sombre citadel dozens of slaves were busy slaughtering sheep and pigs. Fires blazed up highly. Dancers and wrestlers practised in the inner court. Erbou sent couriers to the farthest corners of Circadia. Horsemen came and went... Drunken singing drowned the inciting sounds of the violins, dancers spun savagely.

Suddenly Alwana stood in the middle of the merrymakers, who shrank back aghast. An explosive silence oppressed the sombre citadel. Only the roar of the flames in the fireplaces was audible. With piercing eyes Alwana looked at everybody and said to the livid Erbou: "Lord, divide your estates now! Then ride to the mountains. An immeasurable treasure awaits you in the highest lake!" Noiselessly Alwana left the throne room. The buzz of voices rose. "Seize her!" screamed Erbou outraged, but nothing or nobody moved. Alwana disappeared in the night. Erbou's guests also disappeared, one after the other. Everybody had Alwana's name on his lips. Erbou was silent. Over the forested slopes the morning star shone.

Erbou had his finest stallion saddled. Meanwhile he commanded his bailiff to divide all his possessions, and liberate everybody. Then he spurred his horse, even though at that moment the rain lashed out tempestuously. The gale roared, and pounded mercilessly. The firmament darkened, became a fury of fire. Tamarinds moaned on the muddy slopes. Thunder and lightning cursed the landscape. Swirling rivers sought new beds with thundering rumour. Erbou shivered at such threatening natural violence. Returning to the shelter of the citadel was out of question. Rocks pulverised to lethal avalanches. Tight-lipped, Erbou continued his hard journey with his only protection the voice of his inner guide and his lust for the treasure. Erbou braved the swirling rivers and yawning ravines. Icy air bit with numbness. Only when the evening haze circled the uprooted pines did Erbou perceive the mountain lake. In the dark waters an immense ball glowed with a silvery light.

Awe filled Erbou's heart, and for the first time he felt emotion. Despite his exhaustion after a turbulent night, Erbou was glad, though he realised that all alone he would not be able to lift the treasure out of the water. The night would have to give him advice. For Erbou the night was dreadful. Agitation traversed his sleep, depriving him from the clarification of soothing dreams. Underground rumblings mingled with the cawing and screeching of the night birds.

Only with the coming of a new dawn did peace come into bloom. The dawn was of utmost beauty. Trees were waiting for their shadows, shaking with well-being. Cranes greeted herons, mountain torrents babbled. The first rays of sun awoke Erbou. In the lake, the reflected image of the moon had gone...

Make Music:

"Music helps you from the outside to fall in tune with the inner Music."**Osho**

Discover your own magical sound world. Singing bowls invite you to invent your own music. Be a musician. Music is a mirror that shows you your own spiritual, mental and physical forces. "No better means than music to unite to people of different races or countries," says the mystic Sufi Master Inayat Khan. Bowls affirm that music is called the Divine Art. Be all ears in workshops, factories, shop floors and garages. A circular saw sometimes sings better than a good Javanese gong. Certain anvils, oil barrels (steel drums) and brake drums have a melodious voice. Try to buy yourself some Turkish copper coffee bowls, the sound is amazing. Tunisian mortars also have a unique sound.

Mantra:

Mantra-singer and composer Henry Marshall said it in a crystal-clear way: "Mantras are magical sounds of protection, healing and liberation." Happiness, group dynamics and relaxation are linked by chanting these sacred songs. Singing bowls go perfectly with these thousand-years-old oriental songs oriented to self-realisation and inner peace. Mantras which bring on spirituality are linked with the Shabda of the Holy Sound.

CDS:

Mantras I: Magical Songs of Power.
Oreade ORS 29425 A-B (2 CD's)
Mantras II: To Change Your World.
Oreade CD ORS 52012.
Mantras III: A Little Bit of Heaven.
Oreade CD ORS 55702.
Mantra Music: Sing, Dance, Enjoy!
Oreade CD ORS 58862-A-B (2 CD's).
Oreade BV:

Massage:

Massage is described as the transferring and sharing of energy between two people. To like the feeling and charisma of the other person is important, because massage is an integrating process that opens up all your channels to energy flow.

Massage Phase 1, The Head:

Use for the seven phases a bowl between 25 and 28 cm in diameter, no silica bowl!

1. Let your guest sit down on a seat with a low back support. Remove glasses, hair clips and earrings. Be careful with locked piercing.
2. Put a large singing bowl as a helmet on the head of your guest. A tissue between bowl and head is agreeable, certainly when your guest is balding.
3. Beat the bowl gently with a felt-tipped beater (for ex. Chalklin-Paiste) or gong mallet. Don't beat in front of the eyes, nor upon the ears. Some people like a fast series of strikes. Let your guest decide about the duration of the session. He (she) can even choose another bowl, rhythm or sound. Let your guest have a good and relaxing time with the experience of the humming and warm sounds with grunting undertones and undulating overtones.
4. Note descriptions and observations. The most common reaction is a sense of well-being.

Massage phase 2, Arms & Hands:

1. Let your guest sit down again, without rings or wristwatch, on a seat with a low back support. Use a good vibrating and thin-walled singing bowl.
2. Strike the rim of your singing bowl with a felt-tipped beater.
3. Start on the shoulder of your guest and move down with your bowl on the outside of his arm, in a zigzag or twisted line. You can easily, without any fear, touch the naked arm.
4. Put the vibrating bowl on the open palm of the hand; the vibration will calm your guest.

5. Start now from the chest, on the inside of the arm, in the direction of wrist and hand.
6. Put the singing bowl again on the open hand. Let the vibration go. Repeat all the movements, without touching the arm.
7. Go through the shoulders and neck (fine!) and treat the other arm.

Massage Phase 3, Neck, Face & Throat:

A beauty treatment that uses a thin walled singing bowl of 10 inches diameter. For this massage you need skill. Tiredness of the forearm is not excluded. Please bear this in mind during the selection of your singing bowl; opt for a lightweight one. The choice is yours. A massage of the face with a singing bowl is highly recommended in case of facial paralysis.

1. Lean the bowl on your five fingertips. If necessary balance the bowl, on the inside, with a few fingers of your other hand. Clasp in that case your beater between the knees.
2. Start on the skin of the throat in a upwards movement. Be careful with the mouth; don't touch dents, fever blister or chapped lips with a singing bowl.
3. Stroke the nose and nostrils softly. Don't touch the eyes.
4. Move from the temple and the temporal bone in the direction of the neck.
5. Move from the forehead to the back of the head. For a lot of people, a neck massage gives the creeps and is very agreeable...
6. Go round and round the face and head, even without touching.
7. A careful touching of the brows gives a fine sensation.

8. Use the bowls when nervous tensions are visible in sharp features. It is wonderful to see how the face of your guest will change into a good-looking face with a relaxed expression. Crow's feet and wrinkles decrease, a beautiful bloom makes young.
9. Bearded men have thousands of extra-sensitive hairs that give a massage an extra dimension.
10. Be careful with faces seamed with scars or scar tissue (face lift).

Massage Phase 4: The Back

1. Your guest lies down on his belly, his head on a pillow.
2. Strike your Himalayan bowl. Start, 3 cm away from the body without touching it, from the feet, and move slowly and straight in the direction of the tailbone.
3. Move further in a zigzag or circling line, over the back to the left shoulder.
4. Move to the right shoulder and in a circle (or triangle) around the head and back to the left shoulder. Be careful on the ears.
5. Go back, over the neck, to the right shoulder and go downwards through the right arm. Stop flush with the tailbone.
6. Move with your singing bowl to the middle of the anal zone and move again to the neck.
7. Make, without beating, a circle around the head and go from the left shoulder straight on in the direction of the left hand.
8. Place the bowl in the lumbar area of your guest. Strike the rim gently with your felt-tipped mallet.
9. Place the bowl on the shoulders and strike.
10. Place the bowl now on the back and strike.
11. Repeat these three movements several times.

Massage Phase 5: Belly & Chest

Be extremely careful with pregnant women. (See section on pregnant women.)

Let your guests lie down on their back.

1. Start on the feet and move slowly and straight on in the direction of the abdomen, go further in a zigzag or twisted line to the right shoulder and via the throat to the left shoulder.
2. Move in a triangle around the head and go back to the right shoulder. Move to the left shoulder and go downwards through the left arm. Stop flushing with the abdomen.
3. Move over the navel, belly, chest and throat. Move to the right shoulder and go downwards to the right hand. Hold your bowl a little bit slanting on 3 cm of the body. Don't deviate from the chosen line when striking the bowl.
4. Put the bowl on the belly (solar plexus) of your guest and strike.
5. Put the bowl on the chest and strike.
6. Put the bowl on the abdomen and strike.
7. Repeat these last three movements several times.

Massage Phase 6: Feet

Directed at relaxation and grounding. A whirlpool bath at the beginning of a whole massage is always pleasant. Provide facilities like alternating hot and cold (herbal) baths, soap-free lotion, and a soft bath towel.

1. Take one naked foot with two warm hands, apply sweet almond oil or, even better, vegetable cold pressed oil. Allergic

reactions are impossible! Provide space, without releasing the foot, when your guest breathes in. Provide a little pressure when your guest breathes out. Pull your hands slowly in the direction of the toe. This sandwich movement (dixit aroma therapist Veerle Waterschoot, Haasdonck, Belgium) is a well-known technique in healing massage and relaxation.

2. Strike a good singing bowl with a thin rim. Move slowly on the skin of heel, foot and toe.
3. After every treatment, put the foot in a sock or under a blanket to preserve the newly acquired energy and because abrupt cooling down is disagreeable.
4. Eye contact provides a extra value.
5. Be careful with ankles and instep. Don't touch, nails, corns or rheumatoid nodules with your bowl. Treat the underside longer than the more sensitive top. Bursting into irrepressible laughter is common. Let it happen so long as there is no die-laughing or bad coughing.
6. Perspiring and sweaty feet can give off smell on your bowls. Cleaning them up preserves discomfort on a future massage of a face. Guarantee hygiene!

Massage Phase 7: Round off or Neck Lift.

Phase seven could be a recurrence, in agreement with your guest, of preceding phases. People know intuitively how to touch each other to heal, calm and reassure.

1. Lay your hands, without pressure, as two shells on the ears of your receiver. This laying-on of hands cuts him/her off from the outside.

2. Slide your hands under the shoulders of your guest. Move your hands slowly upwards, through the neck to the hair line. Tip the head of your guest carefully from the left side to the right side and from the right to left. Lift the head very slowly, for 30 seconds, a few centimetres above the massage table.
3. Lower the head slowly. Take your time, minimum one minute.
4. Lay your hands again, without pressure, as two shells on the ears of your receiver. Dim the light and let relish the memory.
5. Remember to give back all the jewels.

Mongolia:

Mongolia is well known as a nomadic state with shepherds, shamans and horsemen without equal. They welcome visitors in their *ger*, a tent they move a few times a year. In the Mongolian kitchens and monasteries of the nineteenth century, people used a large bronze bowl with a diameter of 96 cm not only for cooking, but also for roasting barley kernels over a hot fire until they popped like popcorn. They used a stick and a small square of felt to stir the kernels to keep them from burning. A togoo and a stick: or a singing bowl and a mallet?

Such a togoo, in the national museum of Mongolian History of Ulan Bator, Mongolia, is decorated with the eight Buddhist lucky or auspicious signs (Astamangala): the shell, the lemniscate, the banner, the fish, the umbrella, the urn, the wheel of the law and the lotus. An inscription mentions the name of the founders, Erdentsogt and son, and the date, 1836. The togoo rests on an undercarriage (tulga) of wrought iron (101 cm). Some sources mention that the skilled Mongolian craftsmen, metal workers and blacksmiths were rounded up in Samarkand and taken to Mongolia by the army of Genghis Khan, the lord of the Mongols in the thirteenth century.

Muzak:

There is more and more an acoustic form of pollution. Muzak was invented by an American Corporation in1930. As background music in work climates it is said to prevent accidents, and in cows might produce a higher milk output. Syrupy violins, smooth piano jingles and, in the background, drawling trumpets, provide watered-down versions of sweet hits and sugared evergreens. Today it is big business! The New Age syndrome?

Illustrations

Mallets, Bowls and Bells

Singing Bowls

Mallets, Drums and Tingshaws

More Bowls

Cymbals and Bowls

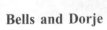

Bells and Dorje

Aum, Ritual and Meditation

New Age Music:

Music is one of the oldest therapies to facilitate healing, meditation and religious experience. Since ancient times man has believed in the ability of music to influence health, character, morality and consciousness in a positive or negative way. Music is still applied to aid digestion, induce sleep and treat mental disturbances. New Age music, which dates from the early seventies, is based on these ideas about music as an expander of consciousness and altering awareness.

Music relaxation is an antidote for stress, but too many slow rhythms, murmur creeks and angelic choirs, direct from the synthesiser, can spoil the whole atmosphere. Critics label much of New Age music as simplistic or bodiless. A reviewer of the 'Frankfurter Allgemeine Zeitung' (Germany, 19 December 1986) even wrote "New Age music is an oasis for civilisation invalids who claim an idyll." In the eyes of some critics, New Age music seems to be only a musical refuge or safety island.

An attitude? An original and independent musical direction? Or auditive soap? Luckily, New Age music can also be described as quiet and inspired music with a minimal and repetitive structure. Singing bowls included.

New & Fake Bowls:

There are no extraterrestrial bowls! Singing bowls are not responsible for the mysterious crop-circles or pictograms. It is a fact that bowls are for sale, small ones with a size of 9 cm and a weight of 80 grams, and bowls of 35 cm and a weight of more than ten pounds.

Tourist bowls can be made to look old by chemical treatment. They are for sale as ink-black treasures, complete with mysterious golden signs, dragons and blank spaces with Buddhist symbols. Only those who want a special fruit bowl or a dish for peanuts or paprika chips should buy this humbug.

Also for tourists, but less trivial, are the expensive new bowls with carved symbols in inlaid metals in three colours: Silver, Brass and Copper. The art of engraving a little Buddha, the Eight Auspicious Signs (Astamangala) or an Aum symbol makes these bowls very wanted by unsuspecting tourists who don't ask many questions about the origin or applications of these fake bowls.

Opening up the brilliant Himalayas for western tourists, mad about hiking, rafting and exotic sights, creates a huge market for the commercial offering of fake bowls, including the fresh traces of a turning lathe. Most of the time, it concerns cheap packing bowls...

New Sounds:

A new sound world is announced. Before the end of this era, new sounds will appear in healing-science. Sound vibrations seem similar to colour vibrations. To let sounds resound, that correspond with the chakra colour of a blockaded part of the body, can heal you. Contemplate the wonderful spiritual energies that music and colour can give you. Here, knowledge of bio-energetical coherence is a welcome bonus. Doctor Hans Jenny (Basel, Switzerland) proved, via his sound-experiments in 1930, how sounds are basically forms. With a specific sound frequency, sand grains, liquids and inorganic powders will form beautiful and remarkable patterns, such as honeycombs and shells, on special metal disks.

The British osteopath Guy Manners pursued about twenty years' research to discover if tone-combinations relax or stimulate our different organs. Sound has a healing power for mind and body, because it can influence the geometrical patterns and the organisation and structure of cells of all living systems. Doctor Manners relieves sick patients by using ultrasonic waves with a specific frequency on acupuncture points. Doctor Irving Oyle (California) also works with this 'sono-puncture'. The new systems bear trademarks such as Somatron, Betar and Vibrasound—A kind of treatment table with loudspeakers for sound vibrations. The guest relaxes in a real soundbath. A metaphor for the mother's lap?

The multidisciplinary scientist and doctor Richard Gerber (World Research Foundation in Sherman Oaks, USA) suggests that sound therapy is a prototypical energetic healing system. Musician Manfred Clynes is researching the connection between music and emotions. His 'Sentic Wave System' proves that sounds have an impact on different levels of consciousness. Chinese Yi-Ching music heals by the five-elements theory. Old medical principles are linked with the energetic concepts of today. They provide revolutionary innovations in modern medical science. Alternative medicines are much more than imaginary magic potions or placebos. The often emotional dialogues between classical and alternative healers ebb away.

Noot:

Chaitanya Deva wrote in his book 'Musical Instruments (National Book Trust, India 1977)': "The 'noot' is found in the Kashmir valley and in Sindh. It is indispensable in choruses and ensembles performing chakri, rauf, soofiyana and other music so typical of this part of the country. It is an earthenware (or metal?) bowl and is placed in front of the player on the ground or on the lap with the mouth up. The noot is used for rhythm, beaten on the mouth and the sides in simple but very attractive tala."

Nostradamus:

Was born at 12 o'clock, as Michel de Notre Dame on 14th December 1503 in Saint-Rémy-de-Provence, France. Saint-Rémy is not only the native town of Nostradamus, but was also the residence of the genius Vincent van Gogh in 1889. Nostradamus was a doctor and a messenger of prophetic trance. In astrology he was simply the best, but he scrambled his quatrains. This made a dog's breakfast of most efforts to interpret them. Had his knowledge been made known, he would have been burned at the stake for sorcery. One of his warnings was: "Let all fools and barbarians keep away from my work!"

Nostradamus went to the Egyptian desert, to the great pyramids and the mysterious Sphinx. He used magic in his prognostications. He used also rituals and incantations as a prophet. Nostradamus played with anagrams, puns and etymology. He has been described as a Rosicrucian initiate to a drunkard whose quatrains are a dubious alternative to pink elephants. (Jean-Charles de Fontbrune).

Nostradamus was right when he wrote his quatrain: *"After that research provides a unique frequency to work on the patients, sound waves kill the cancers, which become weak. The poisons depart from the body."*

Like Nostradamus, the Native Hopi Indians, Edgar Cayce and Rudolf Steiner predicted revolutionary developments in sound applications for healing, before the end of the twentieth century. Indeed, today the finest diagnostic techniques available—echography, MRI, scanners etc.—use soundwaves. Rosalind Snijders, doctor at the Foetal Medicine Foundation in London, published in the authoritative scientific magazine 'The Lancet' in July 1998 that Down's syndrome ('Mongolism') can be detected by ultrasound nowadays. This new technique, nuchal-translucency thickness, gives a reliability of 82,2%.

Origin of Bowls:

There are various theories about the origin and use of singing bowls. The probable origin of these bowls can no longer be discovered, because the original travelling smiths and shamanic sound-masters have disappeared, and their bowl knowledge with them. A few possible connections remain, such as:

1. Mongolian Togoo
2. Indian and Chinese Jala Tarang
3. Kashmir Noot
4. Indian Ghatam
5. Himalayan Kitchen Bowls.

Opinions, A Summary of:

Many people pick up a little about the bowls, even hold one in their hands with a touch of surpass, but almost no-one knows the truth about these emissaries of an ancient culture. You hear the wildest rumours about singing bowls. Squabbling about the existence or non-existence of Tibetan bowls is not necessary. There are several inconsistencies in the assertions; some views and rumours about Tibetan bowls are contradictory and even unbelievable. You will find that many allegations offer widely disparate theories. Until provided with proof to the contrary, I cast doubt on the existence of Tibetan singing bowls. But grant me the benefit of the doubt, because I may reconsider my point of view. Information and proofs are always welcome!

Bowls exist in different sizes and colours. Thin and small, or big and heavy... the result of playing is usually a pure, warm and wondrous humming sound that sings around. You can believe what you want. The result of many questions is a lot of answers, the one is inconsistent with the other. However, I affirm nothing. I only relate what I have heard and read, during many discussions and investigations, from trustworthy (and other) people.

Some opinions:

Sonam Choepyal, secretary general of the Tibetan library at Dharamsala, declared to Dries Langeveld, chief editor of BRES Magazine (Holland), that the so-called Tibetan bowls are of Nepalese origin and are used by Newari people, part of the population of Nepal, during their ritual fire ceremony.

Bowl trader Marie-Jeanne Budé, now living in Nepal, told me, "The engraved inscriptions on certain bowls are in the Nepalese Devangiri script."

Bowl trader Mon van der Biest, owner of the largest and best Bowl shop in Belgium, 'Namaste' at Parklaan 12, 9300 Aalst, suggests there is a link between bowls and the Ayurvedic approach of music therapy and Ayurvedic medical care.

Some Newari people talk about a connection between singing bowls and tableware, or eating dishes for pregnant women. In this context bowls should be used to restore the loss of minerals and metals.

In Buddhism, the ritual dimension is less pronounced than in a religion with an explicit sacramental character, such as Jewry and Orthodox Christianity. There exist Buddhist ceremonies and rites in which several instruments are related: - skulldrums (damaru), drums, cymbals, flutes, shell horns (sankha), trumpets of human thighbone (kangling) and very long horns. The shell symbolises music, to remind one of the melodies of liberation. Nobody mentions the bowls. Buddhist centres in the West apply Nepalese Bowls at the beginning and at the end of their sacred rites.

When talking about ceremonies, meditation, mystery, magic and the art of dancing, the Bön-Pö and Buddhist monks never talk about the use of singing bowls. Even His Holiness Tenzin Gyatso, the 14th Dalai Lama, keeps silence on this subject.

Renowned and fascinating writers such as Heinrich Harrer (Seven years in Tibet), Casper J. Miller (Faith-Healers in the Himalaya), Heather Hughes-Calero (Shaman in Tibet), Réne De Nebesky-Wojkowitz (Oracles and Demons of Tibet) have never written a word about singing bowls.

Tibetan explorer, practising Buddhist and passionate author Alexandra David-Neel, the only European woman ever to have been given the rank of Lama, describes in several books sound experiences in a Bön monastery with cymbals (chang). As a Tibetan authority and expert, she refers nowhere to the existance of Tibetan singing bowls.

Karma Raj Maha Vihar, personal attendant of H.E. Shamarpa Rinpoche in the Swayabunath Monastery at Kathmandu, laughed mysteriously when he asked me, " Did you ever see a Tibetan monk with a singing bowl?"

Mr. Punya Ratna Shakya Onil, owner of the 'Cotton Mask Centre' behind the Swayambhu Stupa in Kathmandu, sells hammered and artistic engraved new bowls (for tourists) in different sizes and colours. He postulates that his singing bowls are also good for meditation, for improvisations and to perform the miracle of instant compositions.

In Bhaktapur, Nepal, where you're falling over bowls, a jocular boy, about 12 years old, told me and my wife Jenny, "I am a master of sounds. The singing bowls belong to the Tantric patrimony of Tibet. You can buy them for a ridiculous price..." Indeed!

In Gantey (Bhutan), small singing bowls are used by restorers as mixing vessels to blend colours. This is for the renovation of Buddhist shrines. This application deserves an honourable mention.

The Polyglobe Music CD-catalogue (PB 844, A-6023 Innsbruck, Austria) (E-mail: office @ polyglobemusic.co.at) talks about '12 metalligen Tibetischen Klangschalen'. Label-director Stefan Ackermann (Acama) told me over the phone that singing bowls once belonged to Tibet, but today they are rare and very expensive. The very kind Stefan told me also, as mentioned in the booklet of his CD 'Bell of Tibet', that a traditionally crafted bowl is an alloy casting with a hammered finish. Depending on the region involved and also religious factors, the alloy used for this elaborate product is comprised of between eight and twelve different metals!

Stefan Ackermann is setting up his own singing bowl atelier in Nepal in collaboration with sound therapist Peter Hess (Germany) and native master craftsmen to manufacture, under the brand name 'Acama', new singing bowls from an alloy of twelve metals. The secret traditional recipe seems to originate from an aged (over ninety years) Tibetan Bön-Pö smith. Four craftsmen need more than thirty hours to produce a high-grade bowl weighing 2 kg.

The booklet of Thea Surasu's CD "Singing Bowls of Shangri-La" mentions: "Over a thousand years ago, Tibetan masters received the secret and sacred art of creating "Singing Bowls" that could evoke a transcendent state of meditation and healing. The ancients believed that singing bowls were physical manifestations of a higher intelligence, an embodiment of spiritual sound that tunes body, mind and soul. Thea Surasu is a Keeper of this healing tradition. His rare *eleventh century*(?) bowl creates an incredible symphony of overtones and intricate vibrations that continually change, like life itself. These primordial sounds interact with each heartbeat; they resonate your entire being at a cellular level to create a perfectly balanced and attuned state of deep relaxation. This album marks the first time a *golden bowl* of this secret lineage has been recorded and made available for the public..."

Consultation with the Tibetan Institute in Flanders and with several Tibetan monks involved with Buddhism and research into extra-sensory perception, miracles and magic in the Kathmandu Valley of Nepal, yielded this information: "Tibetan bowls are only used to bring water to the altars of the Buddhist service. These bowls are offering bowls, without any other function. They are not used for their sound!" Rows of water-offering bowls line the narrow shelves of the shrines in Buddhist centres. The daily water offering is a common practice. Water is poured into bowls; the clarity of water symbolises the meditative mind.

'Resonance water' is the name of a new so-called discovery in healing by Juultje Tatrai (Aalst, Belgium). Her message goes like this: "The Holy Grail project! A new process of healing is developed. During the Pentecostal weekend I received an important message by channelling (Channelling is a form of mediumship; sources are identified variously as non-physical beings, angels, spirits of the dead and the Higher self). The message talks about working with resonance water of singing bowl vibrations. This method is connected with the revelation of the Holy Grail secrets. Resonance water offers the opportunity to influence the energetic system, to bring our body to a higher vibrating level. Unbelievable subtle vibrations gives light-energy a fast influx opportunity, the changing is assured..." There is a tendency in the New Age to have blind faith in channelled material. The sceptical believe in wish fulfilment.

Sudeep Pradeep Lamsal, a respectable bowl trader of the 'Alloy Singing Bowl Centre' on the way to the Golden Temple in Patan, Nepal, told me very laconically, "Without storytelling on the Singing Bowls... there is no money-making!"

Conclusion:

Where the bee sucks honey, the spider sucks poison. So... make up your own mind and remember that the experience of the unique sound itself is the whole mystery! Get your own picture, your own truth. Only observation and use make mastery.

Overtone Singing:

Almost every sound has overtones; these are pure vibrations set in slow or fast motion at the same time as the primary rubbed or beaten tone.

Harmonic overtones, determined by the mental and emotional states of our energies, are becoming a symbol for a completely new way of approaching sounds and music. Man can be a complete and ultimate musical instrument. Overtone singing is neither a trick nor a fashion novelty, but gives meditation a fascinating profundity. The art of overtone singing came to us after centuries in Tibet, Siberia, Mongolia and Buddhist monasteries around the world. A beautiful coherence is possible with Singing Bowls. The nasal resonance of overtone singing melts easily together with the overtones of the Bowls. Listen to Meredith Monk, Michael Vetter and CDs recorded in Mongolia.

Beautiful overtones can also be produced with a Jew's harp (Mongolia, Borneo, New Guinea, Hawaii, etc.).

Paiste:

PAISTE produce cymbals, gongs, tuned discs, rotosounds, soundplates and crotals of perfect quality with amazing percussive sounds for recordings and live situations that require finely tuned instruments. The philosophy of Paiste is simple: "We believe that only a human being has the intuition and abilities to create superior musical instruments. We allow the use of mechanical devices only where they remove strenuous labour from our instrument artisans, allowing them to concentrate their talents and energy on creating instruments of the highest sound quality and consistency. Any automation removing human control from the manufacturing process, is strictly forbidden, as automation is counterproductive to a natural sound and our desire for top quality."

Through the years in my musical explorations, looking for joy and unusual sounds, it has always been a pleasure as a percussionist to use the wonderful Paiste products as creative tools. All of the alloys used by Paiste for crotals, cymbals and gongs have a consistent sound quality. I am still highly satisfied when I try them out. For creative sound colours with a peculiar spatial sonority, I like to use them with my singing bowls!

Para-Foolish:

Neologism for small talk in New Age country. Mystification still works. All you need is money? Even singing bowls are surrounded by foolish stories to force you to buy. It is better to reject this nonsense. An open mind and a lot of scepticism are recommended, because superstition and credulity still exist. Some bowl experts go to fantastic lengths to provide the singing bowls with extraterrestrial qualities that go beyond earthly mental comprehension. Mad as a comedy!

Percussion:

Stomu Yamash'ta is a Japanese percussionist. In 1972, he used the Singing Bowls on his record 'Red Buddha' (King Record EGG900569).

Percussion instruments, which by their nature involve a striking, brushing, shaking, clashing or rubbing action, are divided into three main categories:

Idiophones, which when played give out their own natural sounds, such as bowls, xylophones, gongs, cymbals, bells, lithophones, etc.

Membranophones, which depend for their pitch on a membrane stretched over a resonator, such as drums, pow-pow toms, tabla, okedo, dhola, tsuri daiko, etc.

Chordophones, involving struck strings, such as piano, harp, berimbau, sitar, etc.

A try out of bowls and percussion will satisfy you easily, even when you are not such a virtuoso as Achyut Ram Bhandari, tabla player of the Shringara Group at Pilgrims Book House in Kathmandu, Nepal. The dynamic world of percussion contains a lot of challenges and opportunities with tabla, drums, hi-hats, fibreglass cuicas, djembés, talking drums, congas, bongos, rattles, kettledrums or timpani and other raging toys... A darabuka of Egypt, a Turkish küdum, a Brazilian Berimbau and an Indonesian Gamelan... they take you for a trip around the world. He that goes far has many encounters, many opportunities to change his consciousness.

Mickey Hart, the wonderful drummer of the Grateful Dead with the deplored Jerry Garcia, put it this way in a Canadian C.B.C. documentary: "The drums play me. At best I am being played by that drum. I mean, I am physically playing that drum, but the drum is telling me what to do next, and I'm not really thinking. I'm just feeling."

Mickey Hart tries to cut his intellect out; it gets in his way. He postulates:

"If you're thinking about it, then that's intellectual music. You're thinking about it, you're making it happen, it's not happening to you, you're not of that moment. You have to be of the moment... it's risky business, the risk of failure is great; but, when you get it, it's like nothing else. And when we do get it, the wind is in the sails. You know, and everybody knows. It's a special moment. You're there! It's only once in a lifetime. It's a great creation."

Percussion and singing bowls invite you to feel and to be, as Mickey Hart. Let the miracle happen.

Piano:

In my childhood, we had a secondhand piano at home. I was the only one to open up the lid to play a few crunching and creaking notes. I tried to play it naturally with an intuitive feeling, but the frame of the piano was distorted and pulled out of position. The piano went to the basement room of the boy next door. Jean-Pierre, who was an excellent bass-guitar player, ruined the piano completely.

Today, once again I play the piano, not with a 'trilling treble' and 'rolling bass', nor like the brilliant Martial Solal or Fred van Hove, with their ability to play one hand against the other at a different tempo, and sometimes in different keys. Now, I am forced to choose a more modest 'free-flying' and meditative way... luckily with an injection of humour. I even play on the inside of the piano with felt-tipped small beaters, because a prepared piano opens a completely new range of sounds. A large singing bowl on the bass strings, for example, is an exponent of new techniques with unusual and dramatic sounds. One bowl on the strings of the piano sends shock waves throughout the audience! New music that re-invents itself continually. Indeed, undreamed of by my father and certainly by piano inventor Bartololmeo Christofori... The combination of string tones and percussion is wonderful and guarantees both an open heart and a meditative mind.

Planets:

Planets have their own orbital properties and their own astronomic sounds as calculated by Hans Coustou.

Earth:	G	136,10 Hz.
Sun:	Cis	126, 22 Hz.
Moon:	Gis	187, 61 Hz.
Mercury:	D	141, 27 Hz.
Venus:	A	221, 23 Hz.
Mars:	D	144, 72 Hz.
Jupiter:	Fis	183, 58 Hz.
Saturn:	D	147, 85 Hz.
Neptune:	A	211, 44 Hz.
Uranus:	Gis	207, 36 Hz.
Pluto:	D	140, 25 Hz.

Bartolomé Ramos de Pareja calculated the tone of the moon in 1475.

Playing the Bowls:

Normal instrumental techniques and theories can be taught in the conservatory, but the feeling for singing bowls is either there or it isn't. There are no orthodox rules for playing the bowls in syncopated rhythms, contrapuntal ensemble playing, special melodic features or free improvisations. In other words: just play the bowls, smile and be happy! Dries Langeveld, editor-in-chief of Bres, the leading Dutch magazine on spirituality remarks, "Sometimes it seems that the bowls not only dictate how to play, but also what to play on them."

There are usually five basic techniques for playing the bowls; each of them requires a combination of playful detachment, an open mind and careful precision. Light and dreamy bowls or large and more spacious bowls create their own drone, with long sustained notes and harmonics. When played scrupulously accurately, bowls offer an atmosphere of universal beauty with their own delicious soundscapes. They stir emotions and feelings in a very strange way. Very high and very low-pitched bowls invite you to discover in them new, fresh and strong experiences, when using the five basic playing techniques that require careful precision and much playful creativity.

The five basic techniques are:

1. Beating
2. Encircling
3. Adding of water
4. Adding of toneless vowels
5. Spinning.

Pregnant Women:

Don't put singing bowls on the belly or chest of pregnant women. The womb is not by definition a paradise. The unborn child only feels secure and in harmony when there is no disturbing or upsetting of the inner balance. A banged and slammed bowl that sounds like an open exhaust will frighten the baby. Be careful with babies and bowls. The foetus is not only influenced from inside the womb, but also from the world outside. Keep the intensity of your singing bowls low and silent. Needless to say, it is foolish to attack the vibratoric and auditive perception of a baby with exaggerated vibrations and sounds. Scientifically it is firmly established that the natural sounds in the womb show a sound intensity of about 30 decibels. The sound of a big bowl goes far beyond this intensity.

Prices:

Keep in mind that the price of singing bowls is calculated according the weight. To give a basic price is difficult, because it depends on quality and origin.

Protection:

Incense, aromatic herbs and candles can do little to protect your expensive bowls, cymbals and gongs. Damage during transportation of your instruments is always possible.

Pack your bowls carefully. A converted trumpet case, pieces of cloth and rubber are ideal to protect your tools.

Drumbags will protect your singing bowls. Let your bowls fit together, from big to small, like Russian dolls (matruschka). A piece of carpet between two bowls will prevent dents and bruises.

Lay your gongs always with the front down, so if by accident you step on your gongs you will not do irreparable damage.

Don't let other persons play with your singing bowls without your permission. Nobody takes a violin or a cello to play a solo after a classical concert. Put your singing bowls upside down after a concert. "Don't touch" works as matter of course.

Silica bowls can be protected with paper, straw or polystyrene foam. Don't put silica bowls loose next to each other.

For the same reason, keep a safe distance between your bowls and your audience.

Psycho-Spiritual Growth:

'Psycho-spiritual' growth to another or 'higher' consciousness is possible through working with singing bowls. They have their own stories and rules about developing, unification and acceptance. The bowls help to develop harmony. They invite you to grow up with an energetic force that works on thinking and feeling. Sound heals disturbed concentration and visualisation. Sound offers vitality and primes a process of transformation oriented towards balancing emotions, the psyche and the spirit. The link between body and spirit is clear. Listen to the voice of your bowl(s). Do you hear and feel the unity with the whole cosmos? No need to float or levitate. Keep a lookout for so called 'channelling'... angels and saints probably don't use bowls.

Purchasing:

There are many different ways of choosing bowls. In fact, a bowl seems to choose you! You may find, if you have a sensitive or intuitive nature, that one particular bowl will seem to ask you to be selected. Just do it!

After a cosy home-concert with singing bowls and gongs, a lady spoke about shivers running down her spine. Indeed, only an exaggerated price can stop you from buying a singing bowl when its sound provokes this fine reaction. This bowl wants you.

Tap or encircle a bowl with care. Take your time and close your eyes. What do you feel? Listen to the hovers in the air. Relax your mind. Do you feel power that gives you energy? Do you have the feeling that the beauty of sound gives you a profound emotion or perception? Then buy and enjoy! Try to act always in accordance with your feelings.

As a bowl is played, close your eyes. Open up your mind to the sensations you are experiencing. If this bowl is truly meant to be yours, you will hear and feel the pulsating sound and vibrations inside you. Every cell in your body is a pure sound resonator with a capability of responding to the wonderful and healing sounds of a bowl. If you don't feel any emotion, don't buy it. Try another bowl!

Cup-shaped Himalayan bowls on a foot are desirable objects. Whether they are 'antique' or even 'authentic' is quite a different case!

Once you have selected your own bowl you must clean, purify and charge it to make it your own bowl, to help you in increasing your spiritual awareness. You can wear a little bowl close to your body.

Experience learns that a bowl-lover possesses one favourite bowl, chosen for its characteristic sound and not for the look, ornamentation or value. So, don't buy a bowl as a gift for a person unknown to you, unless exchange is possible.

Align your will upon a bowl to release the cosmic power, but don't forget that bowls and fun go together. They are instruments of joy and pleasure. Don't be afraid to enjoy playing with experiments on consonances and harmony.

Quick Relaxation:

For quick relaxation: Let your guest lay down on his back. Put a big bowl, with a low sound, on his feet, a big bowl on his abdomen and a bowl with a higher sound on his chest. Start with the bowl on the naked feet. Strike the rim gently and let the sound burst open. Do the same with the bowl on the abdomen and the chest. Look for a calm rhythm and go on for a quarter of an hour. This is a splendid relaxation against sleeplessness.

Let your guest lie in silence after a session; a cup of hot aniseed milk with honey does the rest. Or do you prefer biological wine with cinnamon, lemon and wild clover honey?

Qualities of Bowls:

Bowls are feminine (your mother or sister: passive force, the moon), wands are masculine (your father or brother: activating force, the sun). The following attributes apply to the qualities of singing bowls:

> They relax.
> They balance and calm the brain, mind and heart.
> They are highly trance-inducing.
> They remove internal stress.

They help from the inside out.

They harmonise the chakras and aura field.

They create a sacral and poetical spiral of energy.

They intensify concentration and consciousness.

They purify water, food and ritual objects.

They charge herbs, spices and herbal medicine.

They charge runes and candles.

They fortify the working of crystals, minerals and gems.

They heighten the force and power of amulets and talismen.

They fortify clear perception and intuition.

They assist in attuning to spiritual guides.

They support tarot, divining, astrology and I-Ching.

They fortify long-distance healing.

They assist astral travel and shamanism.

They send prayers to people who are not present.

They put dynamism into prayer, meditation, yoga, etc.

They act as aids to inward contemplation.

They fortify affirmations and imagination.

They empower aromatherapy and Bach blossoms.

They fortify the divination of the future.

They are symbols of the Holy Grail.

They are effective in crystal-gazing and hand-reading.

They revive dreams, clear up dream interpretation.

They soften the dying (palliative care).

They bind or create relationships and communication.

They fortify elixirs of herbs, semi-precious stones and gems.

They are symbols of the cyclic energies of life and death.

They amplify rituals.

Qualities of Himalayan Bowls:

The musician and composer Marco Dolce (Xumantra) says "Remember the wisdom of ancient cultures, who believe that the elements of metal contain the seeds of galactic consciousness and that sacred singing metals - singing bowls and gongs in particular - are physical incarnations of a higher creative intelligence. This intelligence can be imparted to humans through the medium of sound."

Rattles:

Everyone knows the particular rhythmic clicking of dance-rattles, consisting of a gourd filled with seeds or pebbles (maraca). Rattles are universal in the rituals of Indian tribes. In their eyes, rattles are almost as indispensable as drums; the prestige of rattles is equal. Rattles, used in ceremonies and in witchcraft sessions, are valuable in many types and sizes; a few examples are gourd rattles, rawhide rattles, horn rattles, birch-bark rattles, turtle-shell rattles, wooden rattles, sea-shell rattles, tin-can rattles and coconut rattles.

The most widely used rattles are the gourd rattles. Gourds of any size and shape may be used. They maybe little round examples of 5 cm in diameter, up to 35cm across. The Hopi rattle is very common. Native American Indians had many forms of rattles made from bones, pods, tortoise shell, bird beaks, hooves of animals, and even the scrotum of various animals.

If you travel to Utah in the USA, you should stop in Caineville, nine miles from the Campground of Capitol Reef on Fremont River. Debra and Randy Ramsley (Mesa Market HC 70, Box 160, Caineville Utah 84775) have beautiful designed gourd rattles and soft drumsticks for sale.

Shamans and healers use hand-drums and rattle music in a combination with rhythmic movements and chants to induce an altered state of consciousness

Related Instruments & Kindred Items:

Orthodox instruments and bowls sing together. The combination of strange and new sounds asks respect for the mystery of sound as a creative being. Feel the holy power in the upper tones of bowls, in the warm rhythmical sound of the djembés, in the primal voice of the didgeridoo, in the blue gypsy violin or in the silent shakuhachi. Listen to dolphins, a screaming train, the wind telling fairy tales to the trees. Enjoy your own heartbeat, the conference of the birds in your garden and the surf of the ocean. The sound of falling rain is as beautiful and decent as a reading of the Dalai Lama, Krishnamurti or Kahlil Gibran.

Relaxation:

There are various forms of relaxation, the use of bowls is only one form. Grow up through your questions to intuitive knowledge. Relaxation and harmonisation are based on love, modesty and consciousness. The simple techniques can stimulate the human organism (body, mind and spirit) with singing bowls.

The inimitable musician Deuter says about the sounds of singing bowls, "These sounds are gentle, almost floating like white clouds in the Himalaya. But they are also powerful in changing the sound environment around you, raising the vibrato of your being. They help us to become quiet and silent. Not a silence imposed on yourself, but a silence that wells up from inside, by itself, without doing anything. And these sounds will create a timeless space, the here-now gate of eternity." Indeed the first and primary effect of a well-played singing bowl is relaxation. There are various forms of relaxation; the use of bowls is only one form. Basically, the technique is always the same; act on forces and energy with bowls and through this transfer harmony. Grow up through your questions to intuitive knowledge. Relaxation and harmonisation are based on love, modesty and consciousness. Men can use bowls in all kinds of relaxation processes to stimulate the human organism (body, mind and spirit).

Relaxation Chamber & Sound Room:

Other names used are: - Relaxation room, music chamber, sound room, healing chamber, bowl chamber, bowl room, sound room, etc.

The point is that almost any room can become a relaxation chamber, there are no limits. Purple or violet is a good colour for your chamber. This spiritual colour symbolises the changes and the magic of your spiritual way. A white room gives the soberness of a monastery. Choose your own colours and materials to create your own ideal surroundings.

Symbols, instruments, paintings or sacrificial objects could be used to decorate and cheer up or brighten the room. A sound room quickly shows the spirit of a home chapel from which you can apply life in a larger context. Meditation and massage become more intensive in your own room. Create a sacred space and place.

Relaxation & Massage, the Seven Phases:

It's my sincere conviction that, what is experienced as disagreeable or offensive, should be taken seriously. There is no doubt, in case of irritation, feeling of sickness or pain, terminate every treatment with singing bowls. Your technique only keeps holding by permanent evaluation. Practical knowledge asks creativity and discernment. Mutual agreement with the receiver of the bowl relaxation multiplies your experience. The order of the seven phases is not fixed, just provide them with love and harmony. You can see the seven phases as a closed unit, but you can also split out the parts and work them out as self supported items. A whole sound massage or relaxation can over-run one hour. Use your imagination and particularly your intuition. Stay relaxed, even in activity, and accept your own level. You are always the essence!

Relaxation with Bowls, Effects:

Promotion of the (energy) balance.
Reduction of stress and involved emotions.
Reducing of tensions.
Upgrading of creativity and imagination.
Elevating of life forces.
Inducing of altered and higher states of consciousness.
Balancing of hemispheres of the brain.
Creating the force to release the past and property.
Conducting energy to the chakras, including secondary centres.
Helping to harmonise body, spirit and soul.
Giving a positive self-image and empowering assertiveness.

Rituals:

A Few Simple Rituals:

Start these simple rituals for singing bowls with a quiet mind. Your bowls are your tools to wake up your spiritual power.

Choose your best bowl, cymbal, gong or bell available for this occasion. Several rituals are more powerful when executed in collaboration with other bowl-lovers.

Amethyst Ritual:

Amethyst (occult: the soul stone) is the crystal of the third eye. This purple variety of quartz arouses a peaceful life and harmonises with the singing bowls. The influence of precious stones on mankind has been known since ancient times. Gems are the eyes of the material world.

Retire in silence. Hold a cluster of Amethyst or a pointed Rock Crystal in your left hand while you strike the rim of a bowl with your right hand. The presence of an Amethyst will strengthen your sound sensations. Every place of meditation can use a cluster of Amethyst or Rock Crystal.

Art Ritual:

After an appointment with the person in charge of a museum, preferably after visiting hours, you can bring a tribute to an artist with whom you feel affinity. Imagine that you can bring homage to Van Gogh or Andy Warhol...

Sit down in a comfortable position, in front of the chosen work of art. Strike the rim of your bowl(s). Through the sound, the painting, sculpture, ceramic statue or artefact will tell you its own story.

Place your bowls next to one another in a semicircle when honouring a statue in a museum or a public park. Visiting the studio of an artist with your singing bowls can be a very awakening experience. Bowls can sing as a symbol for the finishing touch. Obviously, a concert with singing bowls can be used during the vernissage of an exhibition.

Candle Ritual:

Place a wax candle in a beautiful candleholder. Strike a bowl. Strengthen the sphere by mirrors, incense or Aromatic oil. Also use candles in a menorah (seven-branched candleholder).

Use lighting and blowing out of a candle as the beginning and end of a session.

White wax candles are symbols of purity. Watch out for fire.

Church Ritual

Over the centuries, and in accordance with local customs and rites, for ceremonial magic religions have always chosen candles, chalices, chasubles, bells, burning glasses, incense, gongs, monstrances, tabernacles, etc.

You can always ask a priest, vicar or monk to bless your singing bowls. Some people have bowls with them when visiting places of pilgrimage and contemplation.

A bowl can be used as a chalice. Use a bowl in a baptismal ceremony. Walk around in a sacred place, church or temple. From time to time, strike the rim of a small bowl. Don't disturb praying people.

Give a bowl concert during a celebration.

Cleansing Ritual:

Singing bowls, as well as certain varieties of bells and gongs, can be used to help your ability to meditate and to reach a higher spiritual level. A first ritual can be the cleansing. Once you have selected your own bowl you can cleanse and purify this bowl. Wash your bowl in clear running water and allow the bowl to dry in the sunlight. In this way your Himalayan bowl will add to its already high and positive energy level.

Moon Ritual:

For peace on earth, let your bowls sing with the full moon (the silver mirror, the woman power and the mistress of ebb and flood). Let a circle be unbroken. Feel, hand in hand, the high energy of the moon, the stars, the planets, etc. Thank the moon (the stars, the comets, the sun, etc.)...

Fill a singing bowl with water. Observe the reflection of the moon. Shamans and healers believe that the power of the moon changes the water into a powerful drink.

Desert Ritual:

Canyonlands in Utah (USA), the Sinai desert or the Mongolian Gobi desert are fantastic and even holy places to offer a concert to mother earth, Gaia. Provide shade, because the desert sun can hit you. Bring homage to rare and peculiar plants, animals and crystals. Don't be surprised if animals will be your audience. I was one of the blessed to offer a bowl concert to one single, motionless and very attentive cottontail rabbit between the crimson red rocks of Canyonlands in Utah, USA.

Funeral Ritual:

You can use singing bowls in a fond and personal farewell Surround the body, the coffin or urn with singing bowls. Putting a singing bowl, in agreement with the relatives, on the heart or the chakras of a deceased is highly symbolic.

A home concert can round off a mourning. Honour the deceased tactfully in a graveyard with your singing bowl(s). Build an altar in the fields (desert, forest, beach). Light a candle and put some flowers on the altar. Read a prayer or affirmation of your own. Strike your bowls gently. This ritual goes together with silence and solitude.

Masonic Ritual:

With good reasons, lodges attach great importance to the musical filling-in of their honourable rituals. Singing bowls can help to go beyond profane time. Masonic ceremonies can obtain, through the bowls, a more profound emotional and spiritual value. Maybe some honourable masonic brothers can introduce the bowls during rituals. A creative head of the northern column, the master of ceremony, can consult the chapelmaster.

Strike the rim of two bowls on a cube-shaped stone. The left bowl symbolizes Jakin, the left masculine column. The right bowl symbolizes Boaz, the right female column. Strike the bowls and meditate on the brotherhood of man, the wisdom of Hiram and the symbols of square and compass.

Moving Ritual:

Are you moving? Then, you should say goodbye to your house. Strike a bowl in every room, from cellar to attic. Repeat the same ritual in your new shelter to purify the whole house. Let your bowls sing in the name of all residents, past and future. Meditate about living and moving, to meet the spirits of tee-pees, igloos, huts, shanties and pyramids.

Traveller Ritual:

If you are a traveller, you can always take a (small) bowl with you. You will see what happens... A Mongolian Lama, in the Gandan monastery of Ulan Bator, expressed his willingness to use a bowl during his sacred rituals. He blessed water in the bowl and even gave *koumis* (fermented horse milk) to drink. A simple photo of the Dalai Lama sealed the ceremony. Thanks Jenny!

Shaman Rituals:

'Shaman' comes from 'Saman' in the language of the nomadic Tungus (Siberia), it means '(s)he who knows'. Shaman customs and ritual objects are found among indigenous people throughout the whole world. Even today, a shaman is a person of wisdom, with many faces and names such as: the mystic, the teacher, the judge, the seer, the performer, the negotiator and the healer. The shaman is an ordinary man or woman (priest or priestess, medicine man or medicine woman) with special and powerful knowledge. The insight and power lies in mastering the ecstatic techniques of waking dreams, visions and trances. He (she) communicates with animals, the spirit world and the ancestors. Shamans develop in a visionary role, a great awareness of the spiritual nature within all things. First and foremost, they are healers. They can also be fool, dancer, musician, court jester and performer to change and diffuse several (dangerous) situations.

Shaman Rituals (the real world's oldest profession) include the use of trance, psychic powers, helping spirits, animal spirits, visions, costumes, masks, crystals, dream interpretation, divining the future, weather control, mirrors, hand-drums, shells, rattles and bells.

Before the dawn of civilisation, tribal people developed healing practices that still survive today. For exemple the use of sounds and vibrations. Modern-day Shamans use singing bowls in their numerous and diverse roles to build bridges between the physical and non-physical worlds., As healers and spiritual teachers, they serve other people with the magic and powerful forces of music and rhythm.

Rotosound:

Round bronze disks with a slight taper toward the edge, developed by Paiste. Their sound is extra long, warm, lively and bright with bell-like character. Special holders allow the disks to be spun for a peculiar vibrato effect.

Self Exploration:

Singing bowls are refined tools. To strike a singing bowl softly in a quiet rhythm gives support to your inner self. The most powerful means of playing the singing bowl is in a circular motion. Look for a warm and low tune on your bowl. Repeat the playing and surrender to a harmonic inner awakening and spiritual transformation. Sounds are cosmic friends, the most subtle of the art forms, with the greatest influence on our psychic centres and nervous system. Music is life!

Self-Image:

Every specialisation, even the interaction with singing bowls, develops its own self-image with which it presents itself to others. Sometimes objectives, possibilities, realisations and perspectives are exaggerated by an upgraded image, by which intentions, motivations and qualities are unilaterally positive and overexposed. Certainly when money speaks. All bowls are suddenly real and expensive seducers. The question after all is if the interaction with singing bowls, as a specialisation, gives benefits with this exaggerated self-image.

Sensory Cafeteria (Snoezelen):

'Snoezelen' (Europe) is a concept of 1967. Other names are: Sensorial Activation, Ziak-Activity, Primarily Activation, Basal Stimulation, Motorial Stimulation, etc.

The idea or concept is a contamination of "snoozing" and "sniffing" (browsing). In English: Sensory Cafeteria.

A part is orientated to primary activating, especially directed to sensory perception and experience of light, sound, smell, taste and the whole tangible world. An active event with an explorative character. The catchword is amazement. Another part is directed at submission to a warm and comfortable feeling of peace, rest and relaxation. A more passive event, comparable with family affection or a sense of security. The catchword is safety.

There are different methodologies and approaches that are directed at making contact and looking for affective needs. Pre-school children, mentally-disturbed or defective children and demented people can be helped in their perception and communication with adapted activities directed at basal needs.

Associations (a/o):

Acceptation, attention, basal stimulation, be together, be open, be yourself, break through isolation, caring, charity, cherish, communication, consideration, contact, cuddle, dementia, drowse, emotionality, exploration, familiarity, feelings, fragility, humour, inner life, intimacy, involvement, kindness, light, love, magic, mildness, mother and child, music, mystic, needs, nearness, perception, physical contact, presence, protection, prudence, relaxation, resistance, respect, rest, sacred sounds, safety, security, senses, sensitivity, smell, softness, sound, sphere, stimulus, take it easy, taste, tenderness, vulnerability, warmth & well-being.

Music, vibrations and sounds are subtle mediums of communication. Ortho-agogical music practice will stimulate and develop latent skills, sensory perceptions, contact, self-consciousness, mobility, sense of humour, etc.

'Snoezelen' has its own well-founded accents and objectives. The own reality of the demented man is at the forefront. Inhabitants of nursing homes, individually or in a group, can, through the sound of bowls, escape from boredom. Let the sound of your bowls take you to the inner world of the demented people to discover another reality. There is nothing to control, govern or to oppress. There is no shallow approach...there is only you, the recipient, a few bowls and a lot of love...

Rejection:

Some people are rabid antagonists of 'snoezelen'. Resistance by ignorance is still acceptable, but lack of understanding or insight, personal frustrations and puritanism are the worst kind of rejection. They confuse 'presence' and 'corporality' with 'unwanted sexuality'. This attitude can disturb the results and impact of 'snoezelen'. It is important to make clear appointments.

Sensory Cafeteria:

A room used for 'snoezelen' needs restfulness, dim lights, vibrelax chairs, massage equipment, water beds, vibration floor, foot bath, luminous sprouts and blades, pillows, new acoustic music, idiophonic instruments, Orff instruments and singing bowls. These are excellent appliances to calm hyperactive and nervous persons. This relaxation will reduce the use of tranquillisers, break through isolation and enlarge the indispensable quiet and peaceful moments.

The singing bowls await an excellent role, because 'snoezelen' searches for people in need. The overtones that ring out and disappear in silence, can fascinate and stimulate their imagination. Association with sounds, can promote the learning process, stimulate the (self)consciousness and find affiliation with the inner world. Bowls grade up the latent potential of sensory perceptions..

Work carefully with people who are demented, they often abide in a chaotic environment. It's important to make enquiries about possible under or over-stimulation. Look for a well balanced relationship between stimulation and relaxation. Singing bowls can stimulate the interaction between the environment and demented people.

Ortho-agogical music is practised, to stimulate and develop latent skills, sensory perceptions, contact, self-consciousness, mobility, sense of humour, etc.

Thanks to Fons Bertels (°1949), Alimpo Company, Dorsel 44, 2560 Nijlen, Belgium.

Seven Phases:

The seven phases of a complete singing bowl relaxation are a gentle treatment of:—

1. The head.
2. The arms and hands.
3. The neck, face and throat.
4. The back.
5. The abdomen and chest.
6. The feet.
7. Round Off.

Shaman Joska Soos:

The honourable sound master, painter and shaman Joska Soos was born on 21 December 1921 in Apostag, a small village in Hungary. He was trained, protected and guided by the old village shaman, blacksmith and horse trader Tamas Bacsi. After the last World War he came to Belgium to stay. He is now living in Merksem, near Antwerp.

Joska Soos has given, since 1975, workshops and rituals for body, mind and soul. He guides people to solve their own problems and discover their opportunities. He mentions in his book 'I am not healing, I am restoring harmony' (1985) that he was told in 1981 at London some secrets about the singing bowls by Tibetan Karmapa monks. On 15 September 1999, Joska was playing his medicine hand-drum during a recording session in the house of Hugo Ingels & Vera Broos in Duffel, near Brussels. About rituals and relaxation with the singing bowls, Joska Soos observed very considerately: "The sound of your love is even more important than the sound of any bowls. You can use the divine. Use light and love to offer light and love. The power is all in your mind, only your relationship with light and sounds makes your life possible and divine. Let's make more music with our singing bowls. This creative act is in itself a powerful force for healing, transformations and to transcend the normal reality of our daily lives."

CD: **'Friends in Sound, Power, Light & Love'** Joska Soos & Vera Broos, Explosion 96 06 05, Information: Vera Broos, Mechelsebaan 167, 2570 Duffel, Belgium.

CD: **' Shamanic Ritual'** Joska Soos, Oreade Records. **Internet:** www.oreade.com.

Silica Bowls:

A Mongolian Shaman mirror, a golden Star of David and a little acacia branch reflect flickering candlelight in my music room. Incense spirals upwards with the singing overtones of a few singing bowls. A milk-white silica bowl, seemingly designed of spun sugar, sings with a powerful vibration and hover. The meditation-room is more than ever my private chapel, a sacred place that invites you to reflect on these singing bowls from Arizona.

These bowls are the result of an alliance between occult knowledge and contemporary technology. The first bowls, born by this fusion, were used in the computer world as semiconductors in the production of computer chips. This quartz crystal in nature or pure silica (99,99%) is found in several places in the world. It is also used in the fabrication of fibre-optic glass for telecommunications. The sand is dropped into the centrifugal force of a spinning mould with, in its centre, an electric arc torch that is ignited to several thousand degrees centigrade. This process integrates the individual particles of sand into a unified whole. These bowls create a very pure and energetic sound, with a special characteristic and hover. It's a real art to control and manage this energy.

Silica (crystal) bowls are available in two different types: -

Clear: transparent as glass, up to ten inches in diameter.

Frosted (opaque): like milk-white glass or opaline, up to twenty inches in diameter.

Silica Bowls, Playing:

There are two ways of playing the silica bowls:—

Beat softly with your wand to create a bell-like sound
Rotate the wand around the outside or the inside of the bowls.

Don't hit silica bowls with wood or metal wands and don't strike too hard or play too loud. A shattered or broken bowl is expensive. So don't play two or more bowls too close to each other.

Do not lay crystals, jewellery or precious stones in the bowls while playing them. Use a small pad of rubber, silk or tissue paper.

For more information:

Home page: http://www.crystal-bowls-quartz.com

Singing Bowls:

Singing bowls, dating back centuries in their uses, are basins or pottery of various sizes, handmade of an alloy of different metals. Manufactured and traded in the Himalayas by a travelling caste of smiths. Format, depth, colour, girth and composition are variable. Used as vessels to cook, as offering bowls, as beat instruments and for meditation or relaxation. Bowls have a double effect, by sound and by vibration... Bowls exist in different sizes and colours. Thin and small or big and heavy-weighted... the result of playing is usually a pure, warm and wondrous humming sound that sings around.

Singing Bowl Rituals:

"My spirit sings to you. Creation stands at your feet.
My feelings call to you now. Dear one I love you."

George Harrison

Tune yourself into new sounds and unity with the rituals of yesterday, today and tomorrow. Your name, as 'Homo Ludens', is independence. Let playfulness liberate you. Combine your forces in quiet meditation or in singing overtones. Be a magician; taste inner relaxation through making music, composing or dancing. The object in view is the exploration of rituals.

The intended purpose is not the research for banal sensation or occult nonsense. White or black magic, angels nor devils, are not under discussion in this booklet. The only purpose is a little bit more creativity and confidence when handling singing bowls. Here, the study of ancient ceremonial rites is not really intended, but warmly recommended. Be welcome in the wondrous world of simple rituals and beautiful sounds hovering in overtones and undertones. Leave the world of noise, contemplate and think twice about peace and commotion. Use meditation to improve health, self-esteem and creativity. Develop your own powers and sense of perspective. Relativism and humour go together. During the proposed rituals the sound of your singing bowl(s) will touch your heart and soul. In other words you are a son or daughter of the eternal sounds.

Rituals are ceremonial acts. All religions with spiritual, mystical and magical traditions have their own rituals. They are means to contact God, Gods or other supernatural forces and help to define ourselves in relation to the whole cosmos. Rituals make strong connections with our inner world and give, in essence, a pure opportunity to discover spiritual experiences and empirical facts. The elements of ritual usually include: recitations, sacrifices, movements, incense, singing, chanting, prayers, invocations, dancing, smoke, candles, fire, offerings, food and drink, purification, sacred objects, tools, relics, paintings, sculptures, altars, precious stones, images, symbols and secret signs.

For many people the concept 'rituals' call up an image of endless litanies, mysterious magicians, dark incantations, exorcism and witches Sabbaths. Others connect rituals only with orgies and sexual excesses. Wishful thinking?

Smiths:

There is talk about a magical and secret caste of smiths or Shamans of the Himalayas, related to 'our' gypsies and sometimes red-painted British tinkers, who describe themselves as Thuatha'an or 'travelling people'. Those Himalayan sound masters hammer the bowls according to a secret process, using an alloy of different metals.

Sound Massage:

More and more, relaxing sound massage is successful in a large number of people, because sound massage is easy to share. Masseurs are among the most common alternative therapists. Bowls go beyond pure relaxation because energy-power is so released that blood circulation and the nervous system receive dynamic stimulus. This can reduce difficulties and even make them disappear. Bowls don't replace the medical profession. Bowls offer an extra dimension in contact and control of energy. Handle with love and in silence, without measuring up to others.

Sound Plates:

They are thick, rectangular plates of bronze with a strong, warm and lively bell-like sustained sound. They can be played with various strikers, mallets and sticks to produce a wide range of harmonics or overtones. Hung individually, as rectangular gongs, between or above singing bowls, they produce very familiar sounds.

Sounds:

Beautiful tones have a direct relationship with each other. Planets move in their orbits; each have their own tone and sound. All universes are filled with energies from the creative sound. Sound belongs, just as silence, to everyone. The whole cosmos is one vibration, one powerful sound. We are all instruments, even entire symphonies. Let's consider ourselves as charming instruments. How are we playing?

Spinning:

Set a bowl upside down on a pillow, place a little bowl on top of the big bowl and turn it around. Tap with a small mallet of hardwood stick. Keep the little bowl in balance by beating with controlled striking.

Stimulation:

Singing bowls are excellent appliances to calm hyperactive and physically nervous persons. This relaxation will reduce the use of tranquillisers, break through isolation and enlarge the indispensable quiet and peaceful moments. The overtones that ring out and disappear in silence, can fascinate and stimulate their imagination. Bowls upgrade the latent potential of sensory perceptions.

Tableware:

Rational people relegate the bowls to the kitchen as tableware and household utensil. Farewell to sacred objects? It seems that, in the high mountains, there was no clay to make containers and pottery and from necessity the people used deposits of metal. But the Newari people are not known as metalworkers. It is simple to visualise the use of culinary vessels to make music. Pots and pans become drums. Containers for storing millet and brown rice don't ask for much imagination. Metal eating plates and pot lids sing as (unmusical) cymbals. It is evident that these tools invite you to make music. Or should I write... noise?

Techniques:

Singing bowl playing techniques are incontestably the final result of cross-pollination of ancient therapeutic and cultural traditions. Therapist who claims fixed rules on how to handle the singing bowls, are wrong. Be your own prophet! Attending a few workshops here and there can help you to discover the real nature and the spirit of the singing bowls. A personal effort, independent experiments and an open mind, are preferable to acquired tricks. Be your own pupil. When the disciple is ready, the Master appears!

Keep in your mind that you are not practising medicine. For that reason I mention in this book, 'guest', 'receiver' or 'recipient' instead of patient.

Accepting money for a bowl-massage or relaxation should be approached cautiously. The mentioned techniques and methods are universal

The paths of learning are easy to observe and to discover, by practice and cleverness. There is a wealth of talent to share knowledge with you. Fearless exchange of your own practice and discoveries with other bowl-lovers gives great satisfaction.

Around the world, the techniques are approximately the same. When testing singing bowls, check also your own force. Only trustworthy sound therapists and experienced people have the capability to guide you on the paths of creative and healing sounds. They will give you a lot to think about.

The buyer needs a hundred eyes, the seller but one!

Tibetan Instruments:

The most important Tibetan musical instruments used in religious ceremonies are:

Flageolets ('gling bu' or 'dge gling').

Long telescopic trumpets of copper ('zangs dung' or 'dung ring').

Cong-Shells (dung dkar).

Drums (rnga).

Flat Drums (rnga yu bo).

Big Drum (chos nga).

Thighbone Trumpet (rkang gling = left thighbone of a 16-years old Brahmin girl).

Tambourine (phyed rnga).

Tibet:

According to legend, Tibet once lay at the bottom of the sea. Chenresig, the Boddhisattva of compassion, let the water flow back so that a wonderful land was left behind, surrounded by the highest mountains of the world. The roof of the world was born. Scientists referred to the retreat of the Thethys-sea when India collided with the central Asiatic plateau. In the south and west of Tibet rose the 1250 miles long Himalayan mountain chain. It separates Tibet from India, Nepal and Bhutan. In the east, Tibet borders on the Chinese provinces of Sichuan and Qinghai, while in the north-west lie the deserts of Xinjiang.

Strangely enough a lot of bowl-lovers give lip service to 'imaginary' Tibetan singing bowls. They meticulously keep silent about the Chinese occupation of Tibet since the 7th October 1950. As if genocide, show trials, enforced sterilisation and abortions, tortures and more than one million killed Tibetans had never existed. After the Chinese invasion, more than 6000 monasteries were destroyed. Stolen religious objects are on sale in Hong Kong. Only nine monasteries survived the 'revolution'. In spite of the callings of the Dalai Lama, from Dharamsala in India, for non-violence and compassion — for which he got the Nobel Price for Peace in 1989 — Tibet is still controlled by China.

Since the Chinese occupation of their native country, Tibetan refugees have been forced to pay for their exile with trading. Their merchandising of bowls and bells originates from their host countries of India and Nepal.

Tibetan Bowls:

Shrewd-headed merchants talk the hind leg off a donkey, postulating with much persuasiveness that their bowls belong to the Tibetan religious legacy. But Tibetan singing bowls probably don't exist! Tibet possesses only offering bowls that are made from another alloy and look different from Nepalese and Indian singing bowls. And, what's more, they are not equipped with a row or dots in the rim or with star-shaped ornamentation.

Tingshaws:

Tingshaws (or Ding-sha) are pairs of hanging bell cymbals, connected by a little strap. Tingshaws are used in Buddhist ceremonies to summon the hungry spirits to collect offerings. These little cymbals are also used in terminal care, to communicate with the spirit of a dying person, and to exorcise wicked spirits from a house where someone recently died. They are hooked at right angles, for a penetrating sound vibration.

For a soft and bell-like sound, dangle the two little cymbals horizontally with the sides touching each other. For a light and crisp sound, strike the rims of your tingshaws with a steel pin, little clubs of hard plastic or a little rod. Encircling a bowl that is singing gives good results. For a singing sound, strike the rims or strike with a little bar.

Some tingshaws and bowls show a rich ornamentation, usually Buddhist motifs. Often with the tourists market in mind. An actual and cunning novelty is the chemical treatment of the tingshaws (and singing bowls). They are now for sale as ink-black treasures, complete with mysterious signs and engraved symbols. Money can't buy me love? Don't buy tingshaws with a disagreeable sound. Don't use tingshaws just before sleeping. You can use tingshaws to call back someone who hyperventilates during relaxation.

Look out for trader stories about the presence of meteorite and gold; they can highly influence the price tag.

To care is to Touch:

In a nutshell: - There are many kinds of relaxation, working with singing bowls is only one form. The technique is always the same; working with sound and vibration on the lines of force and energy.

The success of a relaxing sound massage increases more and more because a sound massage is so easy to share. To share means here 'to communicate in dialogue'. Moreover, bowls as a solution for relaxation have the added advantage that they are not so expensive and are easily moved.

Providers of relaxing massage belong to the most common alternative therapists. Obviously, empathy and knowledge of crisis intervention are necessary. Bowls go beyond pure relaxation because the energy balance is set free. Blood-circulation and the nervous system receive a new dynamic stimulation, problems with muscles, digestion and nerves can reduce and even cease.

Gearing the activities on higher consciousness to transform energy is not new. To develop self confidence through your singing bowls, you must be aware of the fact that supplying relaxation doesn't make a therapist of you.

Harmonisation asks for love, compassion and consciousness. You can have amazing results with your singing bowls. Go ahead! Keep notes about the time, results, discoveries and observations. Research about sessions, duration and feelings help you to discover the power of your bowls and yourself.

Handle in silence and love. The technique will only reveal itself through experience. The core point is within you.

Togoo:

In the Mongolian kitchens and monasteries of the 19th century, people used a large bronze bowl with a diameter of 96 cm, not only for cooking but also for roasting barley kernels over a hot fire until they popped like popcorn. They used a stick and a small square of felt to stir the kernels to keep them from burning. A togoo and a stick: a singing bowl and a mallet? Such a togoo, in the National Museum of Mongolian History of Ulan Bator, Mongolia, is decorated with the eight Buddhist lucky signs: the shell, the lemniscate, the banner, the fish, the umbrella, the urn, the wheel of the law and the lotus. An inscription mentions the name of the founders, Erdentsogt and son, and the date 1836. The togoo rests on a undercarriage (tulga) of wrought iron (101 cm.). Some sources mention that the skilled Mongolian craftsmen, metal workers and blacksmiths were rounded up in Samarkand and taken to Mongolia by the army of Genghis Khan, the lord of the Mongols in the 13th century.

Trance:

The sound of bowls can bring you into a (light) state of trance, by which mystical and magical qualities gain power. There is obviously a matter of a meditative level of consciousness. The power of trance can be applied as an aspect of your spiritual development.

Tuning:

If you are a newcomer, take your time! You are the one to do the job. Fumble your own way and follow the wandering paths of the Himalayan bowls as a lonely student. I really don't know if there are any golden keys or magic words to play the bowls. There are perhaps tutors who will promise to teach you to play the Himalayan bowls in a short time (and for a lot of money). Sorry, it takes time... and don't even think of playing simple song accompaniments. There are no chords, no chord-symbols and no repertoire in different keys. Clearly, singing bowls can not be tuned.

Ufos:

There is no relationship between singing bowls and UFOs. Dissatisfaction with the regular structures of society and religious systems is sometimes a reason why people reach for interplanetary or interstellar sources. In this context, the past is omnipresent. Transcendental leadership and guidance come from faraway planets and even UFOs. Also present are Atlantis and the priests of ancient Egypt. A lot of information is received through channelling. Sirius, the blue star Kachina of the Hopi-Indians, is very frequently the home port for new (old) truth and wisdom.

Gigantic fleets of starships should float in direction earth. On board, according to obscure reports, are extraterrestrial scientists, airborne troops of the light brotherhood, tribunal councils and twenty million creatures ready for project 'Evacuation of the blue planet Earth'. Of course under the Emperor and Commander Jesus Christ...

Even crystal bowls have, for a few persons, an extraterrestrial connotation. They talk about Bashar, commander of a starship, who communicates with us through Darryl Anka. Finally, the origin of our crystal bowls, according to these world servants, leads back to the temple priests and the travelling healers of Atlantis.

Videos:

Klankmassage: Peter Hess 1995, VHS 49501, Polyglobe Music, Euro Musik Versand, Postfach 844, A-6023 Innsbruck, Oostenrijk.

Little Buddha: Bertolucci Bernardo, 1993 Art Collection 2963.

Living Buddha: 1996 Mind Films GmbH, Garching Germany.

Osho 1931-1990: Mullan Bob, Osho Publications.

Seven years in Tibet: Annaud Jean-Jacques, 1998 RCV Mandaly.

Warning:

Always be prudent; too much intimate touching, ambiguous meanings or suggestive remarks can lead to confusion. The imagination of some guests can run away with them. It's not funny when complaints arise for supposed sexual harassment's or invented liberties during a session.

It's my sincere conviction that what is experienced as disagreeable or offensive should be taken seriously. In any case of irritation, feeling of sickness or pain, terminate every treatment with singing bowls. Your technique only keeps improving by continued evaluation. Practical knowledge needs creativity and discernment. Mutual agreement with the receiver of the bowl relaxation multiplies your experience; you learn that the singing bowls work with you rather than against you. The order of the seven phases is not fixed, just provide them with love and harmony. You can see the seven phases as a closed unit or you can also split and work them as self supported units. A whole sound massage can overrun one hour. Use your imagination and particularly your intuition. Stay relaxed, even in activity, and accept your own level. You are always the essence!

Provide a cosy draft free room temperature, and a gentle and soft place to lay down. Ensure privacy. Ban out telephone, doorbell, interruptions and intense light. Reduce comments and remarks to a strict minimum.

Tap or strike the bowls only with modesty. Tap the bowls carefully and welcome silence. Eventually, use small bells or tingshaws to round off. Himalayan bowls placed on the body stimulate the muscles. Without contact with the body, they stimulate the nervous system.

If your bowls are being used regularly with deep respect and love, your playing itself serves as a charge of positive power. Relaxation with singing bowls asks a feeling of responsibility and honesty from distributor and receiver. Mutual trust is indispensable.

Some people have wonderful trips; they see brilliant colours during a sound session. Other people suddenly remember parts of the past. Regression or autosuggestion? Look out for emotional or unstable persons.

Note your experiences and those of the receiver. Wash your hands before every session. Visiting the lavatory before a bowl session starts is intelligent. Provide a very large and stable treatment table. Warm bowls are more agreeable than icecubes. Put your bowls on a rubber bag or a hot water bottle. Don't use electric bedwarmers for your bowls.

Rubber sealing-rings (from a preserving jar) or pieces of rubber avoid the bowls sliding off. Provide extra pillows to avoid physical discomfort. An ergonomic neck cushion is a splendid idea. Use incense only after consultation with the receiver, and in a modest quantity. Put clusters of amethyst or rock crystal in your relaxation-room to remove all negative energy. Let the recipient rest for a while after a bowl relaxation. To avoid pain or painful sounds, don't wear rings or bracelets.

Clean and re-energise your singing bowls after every massage or relaxation.

Water-Offering Bowls:

Consultations at the Tibetan Institute in Flanders with several Tibetan monks involved with Buddhism and research into extra-sensory perception, miracles and magic in the Kathmandu Valley of Nepal, yield this information: - "Tibetan bowls are only used to bring water to the altars of the Buddhist service. These bowls are offering bowls, without any other function. They are not used for their sound!" Rows of water-offering bowls line the narrow shelves of the shrines in Buddhist centres. The daily water offering is a common practice. Water is poured into bowls; the clarity of water symbolises the meditative mind.

Workshops:

A few workshops can help you to discover the real nature and the spirit of the singing bowls, but a personal effort, independent experiments and an open mind are preferable to acquired tricks.

X Factor:

Singing bowls have their own secrets and mysteries! We don't know the underlying motives of the original makers. It is easy to become absorbed by the bowls and their history; only a small part can be written. There are no absolute answers.

X Factor

Singing bowls have their own secrets and mysteries. We don't know the underlying motives of the original makers. It is easy to become absorbed by the bowls and their history, only a small part can be written. There are no absolute answers.

Yeti:

Did you ever see a Yeti or Abominable Snowman, in the Himalayas with a singing bowl on his head? Then you'd better stop drinking Tungba, the precious Tibetan home-brewed millet beer!

Your Own Bowl:

Experience teaches that a bowl-lover possesses one favourite bowl. Usually chosen for the characteristic sound and not for the look, the ornamentation or value. So, don't buy a bowl as a gift unless exchange is possible. Every bowl has its own character, musical setting, vibrations and sounds. Bowls of varying types, as well as certain tingshaws or bells, can be used to help your ability to meditate or to reach higher spiritual levels. For this purpose, it is essential that you choose your own bowl. It should not be handled by others. This kind of bowl can be a special friend. It will help you to attract and release cosmic energies and to reach deeper states of meditation, increase spiritual awareness, awakening and consciousness. Your own bowl will help you to increase your spiritual awareness. You can wear a little bowl close to your body.

Zonal Massage:

The head, the arms and hands, the neck, face and throat, the back, the abdomen and chest, the feet - all are areas that can be treated by bowls. (See MASSAGE).

Epilogue:

A few books have been written about the mysterious Himalayan bowls. This new, comprehensive and modest work "Singing Bowls-ABC" covers a lot of information about the singing bowls through key words. Indeed, there are no absolute answers, only limited but practical information about their origin, alloys, sounds, uses, relaxation and characteristics.

Strike the rim of a singing bowl in your hand and become aware that the real power is inside you, timeless and free. Practical knowledge asks for creativity and discernment. Use your imagination and particularly your intuition. Stay relaxed, even in activity, and accept your own level. You are always the essence.

Decide if you would like to sign up for a bowl course. After all, the guidance comes only from the energy. Working for quite a while in the small world of the singing bowls, one learns a lot. Indeed, concerts, readings, New Age fairs and shows besides books and magazines give a lot of universal and unexpected information about singing bowls. Daily interaction with the bowls will change your life and guide your attention to your inner temple. There, deep down, is waiting your own teacher, your own sound, your own silence. You are a singing bowl!

Suggested Reading:

Andrews, Ted: Animal Speak. St.Paul, Minnesota,USA. Llewellyn Publications,1993.

Andrews, Ted: Sacred Sounds. St.Paul, Minnesota, USA. Llewellyn Publications, 1994.

Andrews, Ted: Crystal Balls & Crystal Bowls. St.Paul, Minnesota, USA, 1995.

Bassano, Mary: Healing with Music & Color, Samuel Weiser, York Beach, USA, 1992.

Brennan, Barbara Ann: Light Emerging. Bantam Books, New York, USA 1993.

Brodie, Renee: Healing Tones of Crystal Bowls. Aroma Art, Vancouver Canada, 1996.

Burton, Kim: World Music. The Rouch Guides, London, GB.1994.

Dalai Lama: The World of Tibetan Buddhism, Gere Foundation, 1995.

David-Neel, Alexandra: Magic & Mystery in Tibet, Mandala Books London, 1967.

Fontbrune, Charles de: Nostradamus. London, G.B. Hutchinson & Co, 1983.

Gold, Peter: Navajo & Tibetan Sacred Wisdom, Inner traditions, Vermont Canada 1994.

Jansen, Eva Rudy: Singing Bowls, Bikey Kok, Diever Holland, 1992.

Krishnamurti, J.: Freedom from the Known, Harper & Row, New York 1969.

Markham, Ursula: Fortune Telling by Crystals. Wellingborough,G.B. Aquarian Press, 1987.

Mason, Bernard: How to make Drums, Tomtoms & Rattles. General Publishing Compagny, Toronto, Ontario, Canada 1974.

Miller, Casper J: Faith-Healers in the Himalaya, Book Faith India, Delhi 1997.

Nakai, Carlos: Native American Flute.Canyon Records Productions, Phoenix, Arizona USA, 1996.

Moran, Kerry: Nepal Handbook, Moon publications, Chico, California, USA 1991.

Nebesky-Wojkowitz, Réne De: Oracles & Demons of Tibet, Book Faith India, Delhi 1996.

Po. Pa Sgam: The Jewel Ornament of Liberation, Shambala London 1986.

Remnant, Mary: Musical Instruments of the West, Batsford London 1981.

Rinpoche Sogyal: Tibetan Book of Living and Dying. Harper, San Francisco, USA 1992.

Purce, Jill: The Mystic Spiral. Thames and Hudson, London 1974.

Thurman ,A.F.: Inside Tibetan Buddhism. San Francisco,USA. Collins Publishers, 1995.

Communication:

New items, suggestions and hints are always welcome.
If you wish to contact the author, please write to: -

GEERT VERBEKE
Leo Baekelandlaan 14,
B-8500 Kortrijk, Flanders, Belgium.
Tel - Fax: 0032 - (0) 56 21 88 25

Compact Discs by Geert Verbeke:

Empty Sky:

Singing Bowls & Percussion: Geert Verbeke. Shakuhachi: Kees Kort. Didgeridoo: Yanto vanden Heuvel. For this CD only, write to: Chris Moorman p/a: Fifth Dimension, Pruylenborg 151, 3332 PD Zwijndrecht, Holland. ++31(78)6129376.
E-mail: 5thdimension@lingam.demon.nl

Nostradamus:

With bass-player Roger Vanhaverbeke.
No longer available.

Fingerprints on a Rainbow:

Solo-CD. No longer available.

Clusters for Daylight:

Church Organ: Fred van Hove, Overtones Aryen Hart. The music on this CD is a mystical fusion of Himalayan bowls complemented beautifully by a variety of exotic percussive textures and effects.

Twins:

Duo-CD with Guitarist Gilbert Isbin. This delightful CD features gorgeous sublime balladry & ethnocentric stylisations. Geert Verbeke's utilization of Himalayan Bowls and prepared piano coupled with Isbin's artful acoustic guitar work emits mystical qualities. Fascinating tonal contrasts underscore many pieces.

Zeebrief:

Dutch Poems Ria Daems. Music on a Roland JP-8000 synthesizer by Geert Verbeke.

Bagatelles for Gramps:

Solo-CD. New Acoustic Music for Singing Bowls, Grand Piano & various Percussive Instruments. The sound is spatial, organic and simple. Highly recommended for lovers of Himalayan bowls & meditative music.

Discography:

Generally the music, on the following Compact Discs, is quite expressive, variable and uses the full range of music options available to the composers/arrangers. This new music may remind the listeners of spiritual pathways and detail significant occurrences in one's life. The bowl-musicians demonstrate their adaptability to change and adjust the demands of life in a multicultural society. Enjoy the stylistic variations, personal interpretations, creative techniques and eclectic approach to music.

Don't buy copies or bootlegs. The rights of composers are reserved! Artists and editors ask that you don't tape recordings for other than your own use. Most of the artists depend on the royalties, and since the number of copies sold world-wide can be very small, the loss in sales of even in a small number of CD's can mean the difference between releasing another recording and 'retirement'.

The Pig Trader, 'Dirty Linen' magazine

Needless to say you can select your own favourites to move mountains of emotion. Most of the following CDs, combine ancient techniques with the most modern of recording technology, to awaken the sleeping soul in the listener. Some recordings suggest a quiet place or peaceful mood. Take your cake and eat it.

The following Compact Discs represent a musical and spirit-filled atlas. Discover the remarkably wide range of musicians on Himalayan singing bowls. This 'New Acoustic Music' is both devotional and romantic. These multicultural sounds are refreshingly new, even in the simplest setting.

Acama: Vibrations,
1993-Ethic Records, Austria. CD 193 109.
Acama: Bell of Tibet,
1997-Ethic Records, Austria. CD 19701.
Aka Moon: Invisible Mother,
1998-Carbon 7, C7-038, Brussels, Belgium.
Aman Dhyana: Meditation of No Mind,
1998-EMW Music, Kathmandu, Nepal
CD 0002.
Back, Hans de: Gentle Touch of Sound,
1996-NVG Leiden, Holland. NVG- CD02894.
Barramundi: Didgeridoo,
1995-Binkey Kok, Diever, Holland. BK-1055.
Becher, Danny & Vogels, Fred: Natural,
1992-Oreade Holland. ORB 2887.
Becher, Danny: in Resonance,
1999- Oreade Holland.ORP 59142.
Bonsho: Japanese Bells,
1984- CBS-Sony, Tokyo Japan, 32DG36.
Crystal Voices: The Harmonic Vibrations,
1996- CV888, Crystal Voices, Vancouver, Canada.

Crystal Voices: Sounds of Light,
1998-CV III, Crystal Voices, Vancouver, Canada.

Deuter: Nada Himalaya,
1997-New Earth, Germany NE9706-2.

Harida: The Gift,
1997- Nazca Music, Nieuw Vennep, Holland, Naz 9702.

Kenyon, Tom: Singing Crystal Bowls,
1989-Quantum Cassette Link (MC)T2.

Kremsky, Alain: Vibrations,
1990-Auvidis Tempo, France. A6164.

Langeveld, Dries: Savage Silence,
1996-Keytone Records KYT 795, Holland.

Lorentzen, Frank & Virkmann, John: Alpha,
1996-Fønix Musik Denmark, FMF 1114.

Lorentzen, Frank: Harmonic Resonance,
1999-Fønix Musik Denmark, FMF1154.

Marmenhout, Jan: Gates,
1997-Highgate HG 00101, Gent, Belgium.

Marmenhout, Jan: Fujara,
1998-Highgate HG 00102, Gent, Belgium.

Martens, Guido: The Art of Tapestry,
1997-Highgate HG 0020, Gent, Belgium.

Miroirs Sonores: Voyage au coeur de la matière. Soundplates,
Los Incas,
1992-Le Soufle d'Or, France. SO CO3.

The Moment: Music for Massage,
1992-Fønix Musik, Denmark CD1068.

Offord, Colin: Bow,
1997-Spiral Sound, P.O. Box 279,
Katoomba NSW 2780 Australia.

Perry, Frank: Zodiac (Gongs),

1986-Celestial Harmonies 13025-2
Presencer, Alain: Singing Bowls of Tibet,
1981-Saydisc, England, CD-SDL 326.
Scott, Ben & Michell, Christa: Tibetan Chakra Meditations,
1999- Oreade Holland, ORP 58432.
Soos, Joska + Broos, Vera: Friends,
1996- V. Broos Duffel, Belgium. 960605.
Soos, Joska: Shamanic Ritual,
1998- Oreade Holland, ORS58632.
Surasu Thea: Singing Bowls of Shyangri-La,
Steven Halpern's Inner Peace, SRXD 7861.
Tatrai Juultje: Nectar,
1998-Tatrai Records, Aalst Belgium. JT001.
Tillman, Rainer: The Purity of Sound,
1996-Binkey Kok, Diever Holland. BK-1056.
Tillman, Rainer: The Sounds of Planets 1,
1997-Binkey Kok, Diever Holland. BK-1057.
Uijleman, Hans: Journey,
1996- Zwaagwesteinde, Holland, 290313.
Uijleman, Hans: Crystallisation,
1997- Zwaagwesteinde, Holland.
Ven Karma Tashi: Tibetan Singing Bowls,
1996- C&P Music Club, Bangkok. Cass.102.
Wiese, Klaus: Tibetische Klangschalen,
1990- Edition Akasha, München Germany.
Wolff, Henry & Hennings, Nancy: Tibetan Bells II,
1978-Celestial Harmonies, USA CDCEL 005.
Wolff, Henry & Hennings, Nancy: Tibetan Bells III. The Empty Mirror,
1988-Celestial Harmonies, USA 13027-2.
Wolff, Henry & Hennings, Nancy: The Bells of Sh'ang Sh'ung,

1991-Celestial Harmonies, USA 13037-2.

Wolff, Henry & Hennings, Nancy + Hart, Mikey: Yamantaka, *1991-Celestal Harmonies, USA 13003-2.*

Xumantra: Sacred Singing Metals, *1997-Dreambird Music Xonic 0021,CA, USA..*

Zygar, Jens: Gongs, *1991-Fønix Musik, Denmark. FMF CD1053.*

Zygar, Jens & Reimann, Michael & Heimrath, Johannes: Klangräume, 1992- Fønix Musik, Denmark. FMF CD1063.

MORE TITLES ON
MUSIC, YOGA AND MEDITATION
FROM PILGRIMS PUBLISHING

www.pilgrimsbooks.com

For Catalog and more Information Mail or Fax to:

PILGRIMS BOOK HOUSE

Mail Order, P. O. Box 3872, Kathmandu, Nepal
Tel: 977-1-4700919 Fax: 977-1-4700943
E-mail: mailorder@pilgrims.wlink.com.np